Finding Soldiers
of Peace

Finding Soldiers of Peace

Three Dilemmas for UN Peacekeeping Missions

Gary Uzonyi

GEORGETOWN UNIVERSITY PRESS

The publisher is not responsible for third-party websites or their content. URL links were active at time of publication.

ISBN 978-1-62616-775-9 (hardcover)
ISBN 978-1-62616-773-5 (paperback)
ISBN 978-1-62616-774-2 (ebook)

Library of Congress Control Number: 2019945584

♾ This book is printed on acid-free paper meeting the requirements of the American National Standard for Permanence in Paper for Printed Library Materials.

21 20   9 8 7 6 5 4 3 2   First printing

Printed in the United States of America.
Cover design by Pam Pease.
Cover image courtesy of Shutterstock.com / rizanda (Squad of Indonesian Peacekeepers).

To Thelma, Josephine, and Eloise

Contents

Illustrations

Acknowledgments

I would like to thank Vincent Arel-Bundock, Christian Davenport, Trevor Johnston, Lisa Koch, Shaun McGirr, James Morrow, Paul Poast, Allan Stam, Sonja Starr, Jessica Steinberg, Jana von Stein, Matthew Wells, and Alton Worthington for feedback on the earliest versions of the ideas contained in this book. I would like to thank Joseph Rakowski for discussions surrounding how best to appeal to readers outside the academy, and Gary Uzonyi Sr. for his willingness to challenge all the ideas I put forward throughout the writing process. I would like to thank Donald Jacobs for his guidance throughout the book-publishing process. Finally, I would like to thank Jacob Kathman for providing updated data on contributions to UN peacekeeping missions, which allowed for the analyses throughout this book.

Abbreviations and Acronyms

AFISMA	African-Led International Support Mission to Mali
AU	African Union
CAR	Central African Republic
CNRDRE	National Committee for Recovering Democracy and Restoring the State (Comité national pour le redressement de la démocratie et la restauration de l'État)
CPA	Comprehensive Peace Agreement
DPKO	UN Department of Peacekeeping Operations
DRC	Democratic Republic of the Congo
ECOMOG	Economic Community of West African States Monitoring Group
ECOWAS	Economic Community of West African States
FIB	Force Intervention Brigade
G5	Group of Five
GDP	gross domestic product
HIPPO	UN High-Level Independent Panel on Peace Operations
MINUSCA	United Nations Multidimensional Integrated Stabilization Mission in the Central African Republic
MINUSMA	United Nations Multidimensional Integrated Stabilization Mission in Mali
MNF	Multinational Force
MNLA	Movement for the National Liberation of Azawad

MONUC	United Nations Organization Mission in the Democratic Republic of the Congo
MONUSCO	United Nations Organization Stabilization Mission in the Democratic Republic of the Congo
OAS	Organization of American States
ONUMOZ	United Nations Operation in Mozambique
P5	permanent five members of the United Nations Security Council
ROC	receiver operating characteristic
SADC	Southern African Development Community
UN	United Nations
UNAMID	United Nations–African Union Mission in Darfur
UNAMIR	United Nations Assistance Mission for Rwanda
UNAMSIL	United Nations Mission in Sierra Leone
UNISFA	United Nations Interim Security Force for Abyei
UNITAF	United Task Force
UNMIH	United Nations Mission in Haiti
UNMIL	United Nations Mission in Liberia
UNMIS	United Nations Mission in Sudan
UNMISS	United Nations Mission in South Sudan
UNOSOM	United Nations Operation in Somalia
US	United States
ZINB	zero-inflated negative binomial

1

Introduction: Three Dilemmas for UN Peacekeeping Missions

AT THE BEGINNING of 1991, President Siad Barre's regime collapsed, heightening a humanitarian emergency throughout Somalia, in which over half the country's population faced severe malnutrition and over one million Somalis became refugees. A year and a half later, the United Nations Security Council authorized an operation in Somalia (UNOSOM) to help monitor a cease-fire between the primary warring parties and to help provide humanitarian relief to the Somali civilian population. Despite this mission, the situation in Somalia continued to deteriorate and the humanitarian situation worsened. By December 1992, the Security Council used its Chapter VII powers to authorize a Unified Task Force (UNITAF) to use "all necessary means to establish as soon as possible a secure environment for humanitarian relief operations in Somalia" (Security Council 1992). Deploying about 37,000 troops in southern and central Somalia, UNITAF only had limited success in providing a secure environment. In March 2003, the Security Council sent UNOSOM II to the country with an enlarged mandate to help bring peace and stability to Somalia. However, the forces of UNOSOM II also failed to bring peace and withdrew two years later. The UN presence in Somalia did little to offer humanitarian relief, and the civil war continues to this day (UN 2018b).

Three months before Barre's regime collapsed in Somalia, Rwanda experienced its own civil war when the Rwandan Patriotic Front invaded the country from its bases in Uganda. Fighting was intense, but the belligerent parties were able to establish a peace agreement by August 1993. As

UNOSOM II struggled to provide security just 1,000 miles away in Mogadishu, the Security Council authorized a new mission in Rwanda (UNAMIR) to assist with the peace process. During this time, tensions in Rwanda remained high. Two days after the Security Council authorized an extension of the UNAMIR mandate in April 1994, the Rwandan government began a genocidal campaign in which nearly one million victims were murdered within three months. Within days from the start of the killing, Belgium withdrew its peacekeepers and the Security Council reduced UNAMIR's presence in the country down to under 20 percent of its initial size. Two months later, the Security Council used its Chapter VII powers to reincrease the size of UNAMIR and authorize the peacekeepers to use force, alongside France's Operation Turquoise, in helping to establish humanitarian protection zones. However, the killings did not stop until the Rwandan Patriotic Front was able to defeat the génocidaires and establish control of the country (UN 2018a).

In the midst of these two conflicts, the Yugoslav Wars began in March 1991. Fighting was particularly severe in the Bosnian phase of the conflict (April 1992–December 1995), in which Bosnian, Croat, and Serb forces competed for control of territory. Serb militias were especially violent, frequently engaging in ethnic cleansing, murder, rape, and torture, despite the presence of the United Nations Protection Force, which had Chapter VII authorization to use all means necessary to facilitate humanitarian assistance in Bosnia. By April 1993, it was clear that the Protection Force was having difficulty providing protection to the at-risk population. The Security Council decided to declare several places in Bosnia as "safe areas" and ordered fighters to vacate these towns and regions. The Security Council also called for additional troops to protect these areas. Srebrenica was one of the "safe areas." Yet Serbs in the region around Srebrenica refused to demilitarize and leave. Despite the presence of UN forces in Srebrenica, Serb forces captured the city in July. They soon deported the Bosniak women and girls and executed the men and boys (UN 2018c). Overall, nearly 35,000 civilians died in the Bosnian conflict.

These failures forced the United Nations to reconsider the value, goals, and practice of peacekeeping. Traditionally, UN peacekeeping primarily involved an impartial multilateral force authorized by the Security Council to stand on the cease-fire line between two belligerent sides to guarantee that neither side violated the terms of the peace. Today, however, the United Nations defines peacekeeping as "a unique and dynamic instrument developed by the organization as a way to help countries torn by conflict to create the conditions for lasting peace" (DPKO 2018i). One of the UN's primary concerns became how peacekeepers could better protect civilians during war. Thus, the value of peacekeeping became connected to its ability to prevent, or stop, the slaughter of noncombatants.

In 1999, the Security Council passed two resolutions on civilian protection. The first resolution (1265) condemned the intentional targeting of civilians during armed conflicts; stressed the importance of addressing issues driving armed conflict, such as poverty and governance; and expressed willingness to examine how peacekeeping could help reduce harm to civilians during conflict. The second resolution (1270) put the Security Council's willingness to protect civilians into action. Focused on the conflict in Sierra Leone, Resolution 1270 provided the UN's peacekeepers in UNAMSIL authorization to take necessary measures to protect civilians in the conflict zone from direct threats. From these initial steps, the language and focus of United Nations peacekeeping missions has continued to dramatically change in the post–Cold War era. Since 1999, civilian protection has become a dominant concern in how peacekeeping missions are conceived, crafted, deployed, and evaluated. Some missions, such as the United Nations Mission in the Central African Republic and Chad, now focus primarily on civilian protection.

Many international observers hail these developments as important steps toward the normative good of ensuring the protection of human rights, even during the most difficult circumstances. However, this shift in focus creates some difficulty for the United Nations in terms of both attracting members to participate in peacekeeping and then making sure the contributing states are behaving in line with the organization's goals. Traditionally, the UN has relied on renting troops from poor, nondemocratic states for its peacekeeping missions. These states have poor human rights practices and are hesitant to engage in behavior that brings attention to their own domestic practices (Hafner-Burton 2008). Therefore, there is concern that an increasing emphasis on human rights may drive away traditional contributors. Furthermore, even if these states do continue to contribute, their behavior in country may be at odds with the UN's goals, given poor training or a difference in norms. For example, while sexual assault against civilians is not limited to nondemocratic peacekeepers, soldiers from the nondemocratic Republic of Congo have been routinely cited as some of the worst offenders (Essa 2017b). Such issues may exacerbate the UN's dilemmas about how best to motivate its members to participate in peacekeeping and to contribute quickly.

Given these concerns, observers have highlighted that the United Nations faces a significant puzzle in how the organization can continue to promote civilian protection as its peacekeeping priority while also continuing to attract member state contributions. As Willmot and others (2016) note, protecting civilians requires the United Nations to mobilize significant capabilities for each mission. Then, member states must be willing to use the full force of these capabilities to confront belligerent parties that may see civilian victimization as a strategic tool to give them an advantage in the conflict. Confronting these parties puts peacekeepers at higher risk of injury and fatality. These are risks that member states may not be willing to take. According to such a perspective, the UN's civilian protection priority creates a serious political challenge for the organization and can create long-term peacekeeping shortages, ineffective missions, and member state dissatisfaction—the very issues for which former Secretary-General Ban Ki-moon established the High-Level Independent Panel on Peace Operations (HIPPO) in 2014. Since the establishment of HIPPO, there has been a plateau in the authorization of new missions and the provision of more troops as the United Nations struggles to reform its peacekeeping practices to become more effective.

The Three Dilemmas of UN Peacekeeping

Why do states contribute soldiers to United Nations' peacekeeping missions? How quickly do they get involved with peacekeeping? And how long do they stay committed to the mission? Related to these questions, the United Nations faces three dilemmas each time it seeks to form a peacekeeping mission: (1) how to recruit member states to contribute to the mission, (2) how to mobilize contributing states quickly, and (3) how to keep the states committed to the mission throughout its duration. Each of these dilemmas stems from the same underlying problem of collective action created by the original design of the UN. The United Nations does not possess a standing army. To form a peacekeeping mission, the UN must rely on voluntary contributions of military personnel from its member states. This institutional design creates a problem of collection action. All UN members desire to benefit from the public good of international peace and security, but each one is asked to help pay the cost of providing peace to war-torn countries for this good to be realized. Furthermore, no state— even the lone superpower, the United States—can provide this good to all members on its own. Therefore, even though the member states each desire peace and security, globally, they may not be willing to contribute to the peacekeeping missions necessary to provide these goods because of the individual costs they must pay to help achieve these goals without knowing if others will contribute or if the mission will be successful. Although each member state may recognize the value of providing peace to war-torn areas or assistance in humanitarian crises, they also recognize that their contribution to these efforts will not be enough on its own to realize the goal of the mission. Therefore, the member states have an incentive to avoid paying the costs of peacekeeping directly in hopes that others will provide the public good of peace and security.

Dilemma 1: Getting States to Contribute to a Peacekeeping Mission

The first, and primary, dilemma is that the UN must convince its member states to provide the personnel that a mission mandates and are required for the operation to succeed. Before it can consider either of the other two dilemmas, the UN must overcome this first problem. As mentioned above, the United Nations does not possess a standing military force. Each time it forms a peacekeeping mission, it must ask its members to redistribute their own military personnel away from the affairs of their state's domestic and foreign security endeavors to providing for global governance and security. Those member states must be willing to send their troops to dangerous areas before the at-war host state cools to UN involvement or the situation becomes too volatile to manage. Unsurprisingly, member states are not always willing to send their troops into harm's way to stabilize another country. For example, when considering forming the United Nations Operation in Mozambique (ONUMOZ), Secretary-General Boutros Boutros-Ghali recognized that it would be difficult to recruit members for the peacekeeping operation due to the continued instability and cease-fire violations within the country. Nonetheless, he implored the Security Council to form the mission and find willing contributors, while noting the difficulties associated with the mission. As he noted, "The recommendations in the present report [on Mozambique] may be thought to invite the international community to take a risk. I believe that the risk is worth taking; but I cannot disguise that it exists" (UN 2017). Given that member states are often unwilling to take these risks for faraway countries, the United Nations frequently struggles to fulfill the level of personnel required by its peacekeeping mandates (Bellamy, Williams, and Griffin 2004).

Traditionally, much of the risk to which Boutros Boutros-Ghali was referring came from placing lightly armed peacekeepers with nonviolent mandates between two belligerent interstate armies. If the sides became violent, the peacekeepers could do little to stop the fighting or protect themselves. However, in the post–Cold War era, UN peacekeeping missions have dealt with resolving civil wars instead of interstate wars. This has complicated matters further and raised the risks for peacekeepers because civil wars often contain great uncertainty about rebel strength, location, or demobilization efforts (Walter 2009). Furthermore, civil wars are much more likely to witness acts of terrorism, compared with interstate wars (Fortna 2015). Therefore, peacekeepers face greater difficulty in locating and neutralizing potential threats to the prevailing cease-fire or peace agreement. To address these new and heightened risks, the UN Department of Peacekeeping Operations (DPKO) is in the process of reinventing its practices to handle the challenges of dealing with nonstate actors. In response, the UN has shifted its peacekeeping mandates away from traditional operational language to focus on complex, multidimensional enterprises, which require empowering women, protecting civilians, promoting human rights, and strengthening the rule of law within a country. This shift in priorities aims to help conflicting parties lay the foundation for sustainable peace. However, this process requires the DPKO to request larger numbers of troops, which is a significant problem given that member states were already reluctant to become involved in traditional missions. Nonetheless, the establishment of peacekeeping missions continued rapidly until recently. Although only thirteen operations formed in the first forty years of the United Nations, the Security Council has established nearly sixty missions since then. Without significant international support, the DPKO is likely to be unsuccessful in achieving its ambitious new goals, and war-torn countries may become stuck in a perpetual cycle of instability, violence, and human rights abuse.

The United Nations is aware of this initial dilemma. To overcome this problem, the UN offers direct and indirect subsidies to those states that contribute troops to peacekeeping missions (DPKO 2018b). The logic of this solution is that the subsidies may help offset some of the costs member states must pay in contributing military personnel to a given peacekeeping mission. Directly, participating states receive roughly $1,400 per soldier they contribute per month. For example, if a country contributes 100 troops to a mission for an entire calendar year, it receives $1.68 million from the UN. The UN pays this money directly to the contributing country rather than to the soldiers. Because there is no accounting for the use of these funds once the contributing state receives them, a government may use the funds to support its military, finance other domestic projects, pay off key supporters, or increase its repressive apparatus to remain in power (Berman and Sams 2000; Victor 2010). Indirectly, contributing states receive the benefit of strengthening their militaries through training. Soldiers from less developed countries receive tactical training from officers of more sophisticated militaries. Upon returning to their home countries, these soldiers can disperse the information, strengthening the tactical ability of their country's military and security forces (e.g., Bobrow and Boyer 1997). Observers view these subsidies as the primary mechanism through which the UN is able to overcome its collective action problem and form a peacekeeping mission. Indeed, poor, nondemocratic states, which have difficulty funding and training their militaries, have routinely capitalized on these benefits, strengthening the elite units they reward with peacekeeping missions (Kathman and Melin 2016).

However, the UN's recent shift in peacekeeping priorities to promoting human rights and protecting civilians in the post–Cold War era has threatened this mechanism of motivation. Since the end of the Cold War, the United Nations has made a concentrated effort to use its peacekeeping missions to protect civilians and promote human rights in postconflict areas. As Secretary-General Ban Ki-moon (2011) argued, "All of us share a fundamental responsibility to do more to protect civilians caught up in the horrors of war." The Security Council has explicitly called on the international community to protect civilians and promote human rights in a number of its peacekeeping mandates, including missions in Afghanistan, the Democratic Republic of Congo (MONUSCO), Sierra Leone (UNAMSIL), and Sudan (UNMIS), among others. The DPKO (2018f) has placed the protection of civilians and the promotion of human rights at the core of its mission, stating that the "challenging mandate [of civilian protection] is often the yardstick by which the international community, and those whom we endeavour to protect, judge our worth as peacekeepers." Additionally, "Human rights is a core pillar of the United Nations. All staff in peace operations have the responsibility to ensure the protection and promotion of human rights through their work" (DPKO 2018e). Such an emphasis on civilian protection is a massive departure from the original intention and focus of UN peacekeeping, which saw peacekeepers as a tool limited to maintaining cease-fires while political efforts were under way to resolve conflict between states (Ratner 1995). The UN is now concerned whether troops from poor, undemocratic states will possess the interest and skills necessary to protect vulnerable civilians. And the illiberal contributors now face the prospect of promoting a system of human rights that threatens their tools for political survival.

Given this shift in peacekeeping priorities and the possibility that it may undermine participation by some of the DPKO's largest contributors, the UN has turned to hoping that ideological commitment to promoting human rights broadly may attract powerful, democratic Western states to peacekeeping missions in the post–Cold War era. The logic of this mechanism approaches overcoming the collective action problem from a different angle. Rather than offset the costs contributors face in participating, the ideological mechanism hopes to increase the benefit that democratic participants receive from becoming involved in an operation. This is important because the wealthy, democratic states that the UN now targets often spend much more than the $1,400 per month subsidy in outfitting their soldiers. The United States, for example, spends over $17,500 to equip its soldiers (Associated Press 2007). Therefore, rather than focusing on these costs, participation in post–Cold War peacekeeping provides democracies the means to both respond to domestic pressures to provide humanitarian relief abroad and help further liberal norms of conflict resolution in other countries (e.g., Daniel 2011; Marten 2004). In this manner, peacekeeping allows democracies to further their interests and promote the status quo from which they benefit (Neack 1995). By participating in peacekeeping missions that empower women, protect civilians, promote human rights, and strengthen the rule of law abroad, democratic leaders can claim credit for helping to solve the short-term problem of ending an ongoing conflict and the long-term issues of preventing future conflict. Given the UN's new focus on promoting liberal institutions in postconflict countries, democracies have begun to participate more frequently, and contribute more troops, in UN missions (Lebovic 2004).

Together, subsidies and ideological commitment are potential mechanisms for helping the United Nations overcome the dilemma of attracting member participation to its missions. However, these answers are unfulfilling because scholars have not found empirical support for these claims. For example, Blum (2000) finds that there is no relationship between financial or military need and contributions. These results suggest that need may not be the significant motivating factor in many states' decisions about whether to participate in peacekeeping missions. Therefore, though poor, nondemocratic states often contribute to UN peacekeeping, it does not appear that the subsidy mechanism drives their participation. Additionally, though ideological commitment may explain why many liberal democracies participate in peacekeeping, it does not provide an understanding of why many illiberal, autocratic states engage in this same behavior. It is clear from the ideology mechanism that states that routinely abuse their citizens, violate human rights, and use violence at home should not work to maintain peace and protect civilians abroad. Yet they do. Illiberal states, such as Pakistan, primarily conduct the UN's peacekeeping operations. For example, Nigeria, which regularly ranks as one of the world's worst violators of human rights (Cingranelli, Richards, and Clay 2014), has participated in over a dozen United Nations peacekeeping missions throughout the world (DPKO 2018a), attempting to stabilize war-torn countries and provide protection to noncombatants in the area. As we look more closely at these illiberal states, we find that none of the conventional explanations for why states participate in peacekeeping can fully account for this puzzling behavior. Such violators do not respond to domestic humanitarians. Although individuals in these states may have humanitarian leanings, they do not appear to have much influence or willingness to shift nonhumanitarian domestic policy. Human rights abuses, such as torture and extrajudicial killings, are common in these states.

Clearly, the literature has difficulty in explaining who contributes to United Nations peacekeeping missions and who does not. Furthermore, understanding how the UN overcomes this first dilemma requires a more nuanced consideration of peacekeeping contributions beyond whether a state contributes military personnel to the UN's efforts. Nuance is required for two reasons. First, when a state participates in a peacekeeping operation, it does not contribute to a general pool of peacekeepers. Instead, it decides whether to support the UN's effort in a specific location. For example, the state decides whether its troops will go to Mali as part of the United Nations Multidimensional Integrated Stabilization Mission in Mali or to South Sudan as part of UNMISS. Therefore, where the mission is located and the situation within that specific conflict likely influence a state's calculation of whether to contribute to a given operation. Second, when the state decides whether to participate, it also decides how many troops to contribute. Peacekeeping contributions range from token contributions of a single solider in several instances, such as Mali's contribution to UNMIL and Morocco's contribution to the United Nations Stabilization Mission in Haiti, to thousands of boots on the ground, such as Nigeria's contribution to UNAMSIL or Italy's contribution to UNOSOM. The existing arguments about peacekeeping cannot explain where states send troops and how large of a contribution they make. Regime type and military need may be able to describe aggregate levels of contribution, but they cannot explain where states focus their efforts. These explanations expect that democracies and militarily needy states will be more likely to participate. However, contributions appear strategic. For example, though Ghana ranks among the top contributors to UN peacekeeping missions, it has contributed troops to only one post–Cold War mission outside Africa (DPKO 2018a). In addition, not all democracies behave similarly. For instance, though the United Kingdom has contributed over 13,000 troops and France has committed over 30,000 soldiers to UN peacekeeping missions since the end of the Cold War, Colombia, the Czech Republic, and Israel have refused to contribute (DPKO 2018a). Therefore, to understand fully how the United Nations overcomes its first peacekeeping dilemma, we need an explanation that accounts for the strategic nature of a state's decision to contribute to a specific conflict and how many troops to contribute, given the strategic value of the operation to the state.

Dilemma 2: Getting States to Contribute Quickly to a Peacekeeping Mission

Getting states to contribute to a peacekeeping mission is only the United Nations' first dilemma. The second dilemma the UN faces is that it also needs contributions to occur quickly. Many of the issues that the international community wishes to halt are time dependent, worsening the longer they remain unresolved. For example, human rights abuse (e.g., Cingranelli, Richards, and Clay 2014), mass killing (e.g., Krain 1997), and refugee flows (e.g., Moore and Shellman 2004) each worsen as they are allowed to persist. This is problematic because these factors make civil wars more difficult to end the longer they persist. Therefore, if the United Nations is unable to deploy peacekeepers to conflict situations before they deteriorate further, then the peacekeepers are likely to face a much tougher challenge in securing the peace once they arrive (Brahimi 2000). This is because the deteriorating situation will require a more complex multidimensional mission, and much larger contingents of personnel, to simultaneously solve the conflict and humanitarian crises. Such problems hindered the success of UNAMIR in Rwanda and MONUC in the Democratic Republic of Congo. Without the ability to confront the refugee and humanitarian crisis caused by conflicts in Burundi and Rwanda, the UN found itself failing to contain the growing regional nature of the conflict. This deterioration in central Africa helped cause the conflict in the DRC (Adelman and Rao 2004). Furthermore, some atrocities require a significant international presence over time before they abate (Kathman and Wood 2011). Therefore, to avoid drastic, and long-lasting, humanitarian crises, the United Nations must overcome its collective action problem and find those states willing to intervene quickly in war-torn areas.

However, the situations where the need for members to respond quickly is greatest are also the situations where states have the largest incentive to wait. Though peacekeeping operations are often less costly and lethal than interstate war or direct unilateral military intervention in civil wars, peacekeepers still die and military equipment is destroyed (Salverda 2013). States never desire to pay the costs of war, and this aversion is much higher when the military action occurs far from home and provides the country with few strategic benefits. Therefore, states will be hesitant to contribute to risky peace operations. The incentive to gather more information rather than contribute quickly is higher in severe conflict situations where the costs are expected to be higher and the outcomes are likely to be more uncertain because the state's leadership will have a more difficult time convincing important constituents that participating in such a mission is critical to the country's security needs. By waiting and watching the mission unfold, rather than being among the first contributors, a member state is better able to collect information that is important to its decision whether to contribute troops to the mission. For instance, the state can ascertain better the likely costs of the mission, if other states will contribute, and if the operation is likely to succeed. By gathering information about how others are faring, a state can better judge the consequences of its involvement. With this information, the state is then able to make a decision that is more in line with its military doctrine or security situation. Unfortunately for the UN, which is interested in expanding the breadth and depth of its peacekeeping involvement in more complex missions, this wait-and-see approach has come the dominate attitude of the UN's member states. A failure of peacekeeping in Somalia caused states to pause in their exuberance for peacekeeping in the post–Cold War era (DPKO 2017), and, just as this hesitation was beginning to fade, it was reinforced when members witnessed the ongoing, and largely failing, extended deployment in Afghanistan by the United States (Berdal 2013).

Policymakers are aware of this problem. In 1995, US Secretary of State Warren Christopher urged the international community to "improve the

UN's ability to respond rapidly when new missions are approved" and mandates are set (Department of State 1995). Fresh in his mind were two examples in which member states hesitated to contribute soldiers to peace operations. In Rwanda, it took over four months for member states to contribute just half the number of mandated troops for UNAMIR (Bellamy, Williams, and Griffin 2004), and it took over seven months from the establishment of the ONUMOZ mandate before member states were willing to contribute substantial numbers of troops to help enforce the peace agreement in Mozambique (Jett 2000). In each of these cases, the situation on the ground deteriorated further while the belligerents waited on the arrival of the UN. This worsening situation made the ultimate success of these missions much harder for those states that eventually answered the peacekeeping call. Of course, there is variation in how quickly each member state responds to the UN's call for troops. In UNAMIR, for example, countries such as Ghana and the Netherlands led the first responders, while other states, such as Canada and Guinea-Bissau, contributed later (DPKO 2018a). These cases reflect broader patterns in peacekeeping contributions, in which only 20 percent of eventual participants provide soldiers at the onset of a peacekeeping mission. The average duration until contribution for eventual participants is over two years, while 16 percent of contributors do not provide soldiers until after a mission's third year and 11 percent wait at least five years before participating. The United Nations has endeavored to reduce delays in staffing its missions by consulting with potential contributors before the Security Council mandates a mission and by forming a Mission Leadership Team to help build political support for the impending operation (DPKO 2008). Nonetheless, members continue to differ in how quickly they are willing to become involved, if at all, and an internal report evaluating UN peacekeeping efforts concluded, "In the face of a surge in demand over the past decade, the [UN] has not been able to deploy sufficient peacekeeping forces quickly and often relies on underresourced military and police capacities" (HIPPO 2015, 9).

Problematically, the peacekeeping literature treats the decision whether to contribute troops as static—that is, scholars consider a state's decision to contribute sometime during a mission, but not the timing of that decision (e.g., Lebovic 2004; Victor 2010; Kathman and Melin 2016). Therefore, despite the focus on *who* contributes, we have no idea of *when* a state is willing to send its military personnel into a war-torn country under the auspices of the United Nations. Yet this is a dynamic process. States can deploy troops to a peacekeeping mission throughout the operation. For example, though Nigeria contributed troops within two months of the Security Council forming UNAMSIL in Sierra Leone, Pakistan waited a year and a half, and Sweden waited nearly six years before contributing. Similarly, Ghana contributed troops to the United Nations Operations in Côte d'Ivoire upon formation of the mission, while Uganda waited over a year, and Tanzania waited two and a half years before contributing. The decision to contribute at the beginning of a mission, when the conflict is still hot and uncertainty surrounds the parties' intentions, is much different from the decision to participate later in a mission once a cease-fire or peace agreement is firmly in place and the situation on the ground is clearer. For example, when contributing to UNAMSIL at its beginning, Nigeria's focus was on stopping the fighting and keeping the conflict from expanding further in West Africa. Nigeria urged the United Nations to change the mandate for Sierra Leone from one of peacekeeping to peace enforcement and threatened to withdraw its troops if the UN did not quicken its activities to halt the conflict (Pan-African News Agency 2000; Adeyemi 2001). Conversely, Sweden's focus was on resolving postconflict issues once the fighting had largely subsided (Human Rights Watch 2003, 71). By conflating early movers with midcourse or later contributors, scholars are obscuring the strategic decisions states are making.

Observers are also potentially confusing what mechanisms work best for attracting early contributions. Consider how the conventional wisdom on the United Nations' primary mechanisms to attract contributors provides little insight into how the UN can motivate quick participation in a mission. First, the subsidy mechanism expects that the UN can attract members that are looking to gain resources from their participation. If a member is looking to maximize the resources it can gain, it should contribute widely and quickly. This approach would allow the member to receive the kickbacks throughout the duration of every mission for which it possesses the personnel to contribute. However, as mentioned above, poor members, like rich members, contribute to some conflicts but not others. Furthermore, both rich and poor states display a wide variance (roughly four and a half years) in the time they wait to contribute to a mission. Second, the liberal ideology mechanism expects democracies to participate in peacekeeping as a way to promote their norms abroad. Because humanitarian groups push for quick action (Western 2002) and democracies value promoting their norms in the hardest of cases (Packenham 2015), the expectation may be that democracies will contribute quickly to peacekeeping missions. However, democratic leaders are particularly hesitant to become involved in costly conflicts (Koch and Gartner 2005), and thus they often attempt to shift the peacekeeping burden onto weaker nondemocracies and regional organizations (Bellamy and Williams 2005). Thus, it is unclear whether either of these potential mechanisms for attracting participants can also motivate members to contribute quickly. But it is clear that we need an explanation that accounts for the strategic nature of a state's decision to contribute to a specific conflict and when the state is likely to get involved with the operation.

Dilemma 3: Keeping Contributor States Committed to a Peacekeeping Mission

The third dilemma peacekeeping faces given the UN's collective action problem is how to keep states contributing to the mission throughout its duration. Just as a member state can join an operation any time throughout its duration, the state can also leave a mission at any time. Because the UN cannot compel states to provide troops to an operation, the decision of whether to keep boots on the ground is ultimately made by the contributing states. Despite having little leverage over contributors, keeping states committed to a mission is crucial for the United Nations. An operation's success is often tied to the long-term commitment of the contributing states. As the DPKO (2018d) identifies, matching personnel levels to mandate goals is a key factor in missions' success. For missions to be successful in the long term, states must remain committed to participating until the humanitarian goals desired by the UN are realized. Otherwise, a war-torn country may remain trapped in a cycle of violence (e.g., Doyle and Sambanis 2006). As attrition occurs, the likelihood of success decreases because the mandate cannot be realized. In Rwanda, for example, Belgium's withdrawal of its troops severely hampered UNAMIR's ability to keep the peace and end the ongoing genocide (Meisler 1994). A former major-general of UNAMIR, Roméo Dallaire (2009), considers Belgium's early withdrawal and the United Nations' inability to find another significant troop contributor as one of the determining factors in UNAMIR's failure to achieve its mandate. Similarly, over 60 percent of contributing states withdrew from the United Nations Organization Mission in the Democratic Republic of the Congo (MONUC) more than two years before the mission concluded. In response, the UN attempted to reorganize and strengthen its presence in the DRC with a new mission—MONUSCO—but has continued to struggle in keeping members committed and realizing the goals of its mandate (e.g., Security Council 2017).

The experiences of UNAMIR and MONUC are not unique. Rather, over 45 percent of all contributors withdraw from UN peacekeeping missions before the operation concludes (Kathman 2013). Retention issues have become increasingly important in the post–Cold War era. After the end of a civil war, peacekeepers now help deliver humanitarian aid, empower women, prevent crime, promote human rights, protect civilians, and strengthen the rule of law in the postconflict country (DPKO 2018h). Each of these activities stretches a peacekeeping force's abilities and capacity because the troops must provide these services while continuing to perform their basic functions of monitoring cease-fires and patrolling former combatants as they disarm and reintegrate back into society. The UN Security Council has recognized the strain these additional functions create and has called on its members to provide larger numbers of personnel to its ongoing missions, as in MONUSCO (Security Council 2010). However, this response to retention issues—expanding mandates and relying more heavily on its members' continued contributions—places the Security Council in a difficult situation, in that this proposed solution requires more of the states that have remained committed to peacekeeping rather than helping to relieve their burden. Further increasing the burden of these participants risks alienating them and causing their early withdrawal.

The tension between the ever-expanding post–Cold War peacekeeping mandates and the difficulties of keeping members engaged in missions to help realize the long-term goals of the operations has not been lost on the United Nations' leadership. Over the past decade, the UN has engaged in two efforts to revamp its peacekeeping practices and increase the success-fulness of its missions. The first effort was the New Horizon process, which was initiated in 2009. The goals of this process were to "assess the major policy and strategy dilemmas facing UN Peacekeeping today and over the coming years; and reinvigorate the ongoing dialogue with stake-holders on possible solutions to better calibrate UN Peacekeeping to meet current and future requirements" (DPKO 2018g). From the New Horizon process, it became clear that member states' calculations were being neglected in the peace operation planning stage. The New Horizon report urged dialogue between "all stakeholders in the global peacekeeping part-nership" to "help crystallize a common vision." As a result of the New Horizon process, then–Secretary-General Ban Ki-moon established the

High-Level Independent Panel on UN Peace Operations in 2014. After a year of investigation, this panel concluded that

> a number of peace operations today are deployed in an environment where there is little or no peace to keep. In many settings today, the strain on their operational capabilities and support systems is showing, and political support is often stretched thin. There is a clear sense of a widening gap between what is being asked of United Nations peace operations today and what they are able to deliver. That gap can be, must be, narrowed to ensure that the Organization's peace operations are able to respond effectively and appropriately to the challenges to come. With a current generation of conflicts proving difficult to resolve and with new ones emerging, it is essential that United Nations peace operations, along with regional and other partners, combine their respective comparative advantages and unite their strengths in the service of peace and security. (HIPPO 2015, 9)

From this conclusion, and in conjunction with other suggested reforms, the panel recommended that the Security Council scale back what it asks of member states in a given mission's mandate (HIPPO 2015, 16–19). The hope is that if missions are better funded, have clearer mandates, and ask less of contributing states, then more member states will participate and remain committed to peacekeeping. However, these recommendations face a similar problem as previous academic explanations for why a state participates in peacekeeping, in that each tells us little about why a state remains committed to the operation. Each maintains the premise that a state's calculation for why it is participating at the beginning of the mission remains constant throughout the duration of the mission. This premise suggests that if a state found the conditions and terms of the operation favorable in the first month of the mission, it is likely to find the situation on the ground and the terms of the mandate favorable in the fifth year of the operation. This is problematic because the incentive to participate originally in a proposed mission may be quite different from the incentive to remain involved. Domestic political situations, international pressures, and conditions in the field each can change over the course of a mission. These changes alter the decision-making of a member state. If the conflict conditions worsen, for example, then the initial motivations for participating in the mission may not be enough to keep a state committed to the operation, even if the mandate does not require much of the deployed personnel.

Patterns in peacekeepers' deployment underscore the difficulty current thinking on contributor retention has in explaining how long states stay committed to a given operation. For example, among the UN's poorest contributors, which should benefit disproportionately from the standardized reimbursement rate, wide variance exists in how long each state stays committed to a given mission. Though the mean duration of participation for these states is forty-one months, there is also a standard deviation of forty-one months in their contribution durations. Sierra Leone, for instance, stayed in Liberia for two months as part of UNMIL, whereas Ethiopia remained committed to UNMIL for over twelve years, despite both countries having real GDP per capita of about $700. Democratic participants display a similarly wide variance in how long they remain committed to a given operation. For example, the Netherlands participated in UNMIL for three months, while Finland remained committed for twelve years. These patterns suggest that a new explanation is needed for why some states withdraw sooner from peacekeeping missions than others. Connected to the discussion of the UN's other two dilemmas in peacekeeping, I propose that observers and scholars of peacekeeping must consider conflict- and mission-specific factors that influence a member state's calculations of whether, when, and how long to become involved in a UN peacekeeping mission.

Outlining a New Argument

How can the United Nations overcome these three dilemmas? Which states participate, contribute the most, become involved quickly, and remain committed to a mission? As discussed above, the United Nations has shifted its peacekeeping rhetoric and focus to the promotion of human rights and the protection of civilians in the post–Cold War era. Furthermore, if the Security Council and DPKO adopt many of HIPPO's proposed changes, then peacekeeping will move even more in this direction, with civilian protection at the forefront of the UN's priorities. However, despite the UN's humanitarian rhetoric, I argue that participation in peacekeeping plays a role similar to military intervention for many states, in that it provides the UN's members with the opportunity to achieve their desired goals in other states through armed participation in a target state's domestic politics. The similarities between military intervention and peacekeeping operations have increased in recent years as the Security Council has authorized more robust peacekeeping missions that allow troops to use all necessary means to achieve their goals (Tardy 2011), and it has emphasized tying the missions' goals to the political process and outcomes of the combatant's conflict bargaining (HIPPO 2015). The benefit of pursuing these goals through United Nations peacekeeping, rather than unilateral intervention, is that the states are able to share the burden of the intervention with the other contributors. Participants and the relevant UN departments share troop levels, communications, and logistical planning. Furthermore, the United Nations compensates the state for providing its personnel. Although this compensation may not fully offset the cost of participation, it helps reduce the overall cost.

Entering another state under the auspices of the United Nations, rather than unilaterally, also helps reduce the reputational costs of the militarized action for the participants. Intervening uninvited in another country's domestic affairs is against international law and norms (e.g., Roberts 1993). Such unilateral intervention raises criticism and possible sanction against the offending state and places the full burden of the military action on the state's shoulders. For instance, when Russia intervened in Ukraine due to the 2014 secession of the Crimean province, it received harsh criticism from the European Union and United States for its unilateral action (Dunham 2014). Participation in United Nations peacekeeping helps reduce such reputational costs by giving a state the legitimizing cover of UN authorization to send troops into another country (Boutros-Ghali 1999). Having the UN's blessing for the military action also helps reduce the risk of legal action before the International Criminal Court by removing concerns of aggressive war. Thus, when a state uses UN peacekeeping as a way to pursue its foreign policy goals, this helps reduce both the state's military and reputational costs for action while simultaneously helping it appear to be a good citizen of the international community for its work in assisting to bring peace to a war-torn country.

By reducing the costs associated with deploying troops abroad, UN peacekeeping helps increase a state's opportunity to pursue its goals in another country. Despite these benefits, not all states will find participation attractive, for two reasons. First, a state may lack a motive to participate. To intervene abroad, a state must have both opportunity and a motive (Siverson and Starr 1990). Although the authorization of a peacekeeping mission may help provide opportunity, if a state does not find intervention in a particular conflict beneficial for its foreign policy goals, it is unlikely to risk its personnel abroad because the return from such action is low. Second, a state may not participate in a UN mission even if it has a motive to operate within the target country. This is because its goals may not be compatible with the UN's objectives or peacekeeping mandate for the war-torn country. By creating a mandate and highlighting particular goals and preferred outcomes, the United Nations effectively limits the full range of policy objectives and behaviors allowable to its contributing members within the target country. Although the UN faces command-and-control issues of its members' military forces once they enter the target country, its increased attention to monitoring and punishing disobedient personnel works to constrain some potentially insidious member state behavior (Leck 2009). Together, members' lack of interest and UN policing of on-the-ground behavior reduces the pool of states that are willing to contribute to a given mission.

I posit that a state's motive to participate in post–Cold War United Nations peacekeeping missions stems from how it evaluates the direct benefits of intervening in a given conflict. Conflict-specific factors—such as arms flows, conflict contagion, illicit trade or smuggling, and refugee inflows—are more important for a state's decision whether to participate in a given mission than are larger international concerns of peace and stability or global humanitarian issues. However, the state's calculations surrounding these conflict concerns are filtered through the lens of the UN's post–Cold War humanitarian rhetoric and focus on civilian protection. This means that when a state is directly and negatively affected by an ongoing conflict, it will look for the most effective policy solutions to end these externalities at the lowest cost. When the state's goals in ending these conflict-specific externalities converge with the United Nations' stated goals in forming a given peacekeeping mission, the state becomes more likely to participate, contribute substantially, and become involved quickly.

Given the United Nations' post–Cold War focus on protecting civilians, member states concerned with refugee inflows from the conflict are those states most likely to see participating in the peacekeeping mission as beneficial. States seek to prevent conflict externalities, and especially refugee inflows, because they expect such inflows to drain resources, spread unrest, and create conflict within their borders. States intervene to stop outflows in hopes of avoiding the costlier consequences of these conflict externalities in the future. For potential contributors, refugees become the focus because they fit best within the UN's modern peacekeeping focus on civilian protection. Civilians who are abused or threatened with the violence of war are those who are most likely to become refugees (e.g., Uzonyi 2014). Reducing the factors that lead to forced migration is crucial for nearby states that fear refugee inflows. By alleviating the causes or mitigating the effects of abuse or violence, states help reduce the likelihood that civilians in or near the conflict zone will look for protection and shelter outside their home country. From the contributor's perspective, protecting civilians through peacekeeping is thus useful in helping reduce the potential flows of refugees into its territory. From the UN's perspective, protecting the civilian population through its peacekeeping missions accomplishes the organization's post–Cold War objectives of prioritizing limiting the civilian costs of war and helping establish human rights in war-torn countries (Hultman, Kathman, and Shannon 2013). Therefore, though the incentive to protect civilians in war zones may differ between a member state and the UN as an organizational body, these differing objectives help reinforce one another and lead to an outcome that both the member state and UN desire.

By working to protect civilians as part of a UN mission, the state helps reduce the refugee inflows it fears. In post–Cold War operations, peacekeepers engage in three primary activities (DPKO 2018h). First, they engage in the more traditional peacekeeping practice of creating a barrier between the warring parties. This barrier helps reduce the likelihood of accidents or intentional actions that can create fear between the sides and return the country to civil war. It also reduces the direct threat civilians in the area fear from combat violence. As the area stabilizes, fewer individuals are likely to leave the homes, places, and societies they know for the unknowns of refugee camps. Second, peacekeepers separate the belligerents from the civilian population. Separating combatants from civilians reduces the likelihood that either party will prey on the civilian population. A party cannot easily strike at its enemy's population nor can it forcibly recruit civilians or appropriate their belongings for their military efforts. When the civilians are protected from predation from either side, they will find fewer benefits from leaving the area or country. Finally, the peacekeepers help deliver aid to displaced and needy populations. This food and monetary aid helps keep the population from migrating further from the conflict zone and reduces the likelihood that they will flee across an international border. Together, these three practices help reduce the push factors that drive forced migration (Moore and Shellman 2004), and they thus also achieve the member state's goals of reducing refugees and other externalities from flowing across its borders.

The UN's peacekeeping dilemmas stem from the collective action problem that its institutional design creates in relying on voluntary contributions by its members. Overcoming collective action often requires actors to receive selective benefits for their participation (Olson 1965). Stopping externalities is a selective benefit that helps states overcome the collective action problem associated with peacekeeping. This suggests that the value that a given state places on preventing refugee inflows from a specific conflict helps clarify which states are likely to participate in which mission, when they are likely to get involved, and how much they will contribute. A state is more likely to contribute to peacekeeping missions in situations from which it is experiencing refugee inflows because its actions in this conflict will have the most direct effect on preventing the externalities it fears. The state is likely to contribute more troops to peacekeeping missions in situations from which it is experiencing higher volumes of refugee inflows because it feels pressure to dedicate the additional personnel needed to stem the flows more quickly in these situations than when it is receiving few externalities. And though states may contribute to a mission for several reasons, a state is likely to commit troops more quickly to peacekeeping missions in situations from which it is experiencing higher volumes of refugee inflows because these concerns are more pressing than those that are not directly tied to the conflict.

Note that this is an instrumental view of peacekeeping. States use peacekeeping to accomplish specific foreign policy goals. In particular, they use the blue helmet of UN peacekeeping as a legitimizing cover to affect domestic change in another state. This is a dyadic argument. Each time a peacekeeping mission is authorized, the member states consider whether participation in that mission will be advantageous for their goals. The member states make this determination based on the consequences they face from each given mission, not necessarily the international situation. The state is concerned with the refugees it directly faces from that specific conflict, not the global humanitarian crisis the conflict may create more broadly. This means that a contributing state has certain expectations about what it hopes to accomplish by working through the UN apparatus. Helping to protect the at-risk population by providing peacekeepers should result in lower flows of refugees to the contributing state. Though UN peacekeeping missions often succeed in reducing externality flows and stabilizing regions (Beardsley 2011), failures do occur (e.g., MONUC). If working through the United Nations fails to stem the inflow of refugees the state experiences once joining the mission, a state will update its expectations about the value of participating in the operation. In situations where the state continues to experience refugee flows from the managed conflict, it will likely look for options outside the United Nations to accomplish its goals. Therefore, I expect that a state is likely to withdraw more quickly from a peacekeeping mission in situations when it continues to receive higher volumes of refugee inflows despite the peacekeepers' presence. This means that while stopping refugee inflows provides a mechanism for the member states to overcome the collective action problem, this same incentive can also break apart a mission.

Contributions of This Book

My argument makes two primary contributions to our understanding of peacekeeping. First, this book contributes to our understanding of peace-keeping by considering conflict- and mission-specific incentives for states to become involved in peacekeeping, thus providing an explanation that helps solve a broader set of dilemmas that the United Nations faces in peace-keeping beyond *who* participates. Most research on peacekeeping tends to either give broad description of how missions operate (e.g., Bellamy, Williams, and Griffin 2004) or focus on whether peacekeeping is a suc-cessful conflict-management tool (e.g., Fortna 2008). When scholars focus on troop contributions, they tend to focus on who contributes to missions (e.g., Berman and Sams 2000; Blum 2000; Bobrow and Boyer 1997; Daniel, Taft, and Wiharta 2008; Neack 1995; Victor 2010). As discussed above, this is only one part of the larger contributor question, and it is only the first of the United Nations' three peacekeeping dilemmas. By focusing only on the "who" question of the contribution puzzle, this body of literature has provided skewed answers and only a partial view of the larger conflict-management context. By considering how the UN's institutional design has led to a collective action problem in maintaining international peace and security, I am able to better explore the interconnectedness of the three peacekeeping dilemmas. Furthermore, I move beyond the suggested institutional and normative explanations for peacekeeping contributions to consider conflict-specific benefits of missions, which makes a clearer connection between the UN's goals in providing peacekeeping and its member states' foreign policy objectives. Drawing this connection thus helps to predict not only who is most likely to send support (those fearing refugee inflows) but also where they send assistance (to the specific conflict area producing the externalities), when they become involved (once the inflows become pressing), the size of the contribution (increasing relative to the inflows), and when they leave a mission (if the mission fails to pre-vent further inflows).

Second, in this book I contribute to the study of peacekeeping by underscoring that the decision to participate in peacekeeping is strategic and often narrowly debated around issues dealing with a specific conflict or mission rather than global concerns about international peace and security. Observers expect civil wars with significant humanitarian crises to attract greater attention than other conflicts for two main reasons. First, as the crisis worsens, it will become a greater risk to regional or international peace and security. Because states fear such instability, they will be willing to contribute to the goal of preventing further crises to avoid conflict contagion. Second, the growing norm of civilian protection within the United Nations influences its members' decision-making. Given that humanitarian crises increase threats to civilian populations as they worsen, the UN's members will work together to manage the conflict and protect the at-risk population. However, contrary to these expectations (e.g., Bove and Elia 2011; Choi 2013), I find that large-scale humanitarian crises do not increase participation in peace operations. Rather, direct externalities from the conflict help determine which states participate in a mission and when. This finding suggests two important considerations. First, norms of civilian protection at the UN organizational level may not filter down to the member states. Rather, domestic considerations about the consequences of specific conflicts and the value of peacekeeping as a tool in those situations largely determines member behavior. Second, when large-scale humanitarian crises attract a large number of contributors, this likely occurs because several states are directly affected by the conflict. For example, UNAMIR and the effect of the Rwandan genocide on the states in the African Great Lakes Region and United Nations Interim Administration Mission in Kosovo and the effect of the Yugoslav and Kosovo crises on European states each resulted in these crises attracting much international action.

These contributions to the peacekeeping literature also raise important insights into issues that peacekeeping is meant to address. For example, even though the secretary-general, Security Council, and Department of Peacekeeping Operations each often uses humanitarian language and invokes the need to promote human rights in war-torn countries, UN peacekeepers are regularly at the center of abuse scandals (e.g., Anderlini 2017; Essa 2017a). Similarly, though the United Nations promotes democratic government and inclusion in postconflict politics, target states rarely democratize after a peacekeeping mission (Bueno de Mesquita and Downs 2006). Why do the UN's efforts at democratization, postconflict stabilization, and the protection of human rights often fail? The lessons learned from this analysis highlight the divergence of goals between the UN's institutional actors and its member states. Because members participate in peacekeeping to achieve their own foreign policy objectives, and often leave when these goals are failing, they have little incentive to directly pursue the UN's other goals. Such goals often require a much longer-term investment of time and resources than members are willing to provide. These patterns further underscore Landman's (2005) claims that the protection of human rights in foreign policy remains based primarily on geostrategic interests than on global norms.

Road Map for This Book

The remainder of this book is divided into three chapters. Chapter 2 develops the logic of peacekeeping as externality prevention. I consider the benefits that a state gains from stabilizing various war zones. I then connect those conflict- and mission-specific benefits to a state's value for peacekeeping. Following this logic, I trace how the incentive to prevent refugees influences a state's decisions concerning how many peacekeepers to provide, how quickly to participate, and how long to stay committed to the effort. I provide case studies on US contributions to the United Nations Mission in Haiti and Tanzania's involvement in MONUC in the Democratic Republic of Congo to buttress my argument.

Chapter 3 provides empirical tests of my arguments on all post–Cold War UN peacekeeping missions. Chapter 3 first focuses on whether, where, and how much a state contributes to a peacekeeping mission. Next, it examines how quickly a state becomes involved in a given mission, and finally it tests my arguments in relation to when a state withdraws from an operation. These empirical tests provide strong support for my argument. UN member states often use the organization's peacekeeping missions as a way to stem conflict externalities into their territory. If the mission fails to provide the desired outcome, the state is likely to leave the operation and look for options elsewhere. I also evaluate my econometric results alongside case studies of member state participation in UNMIS in Sudan and the United Nations Multidimensional Integrated Stabilization Mission in Mali.

Chapter 4 is the book's conclusion. In this final chapter, I consider the implications of my theory and findings. Narrowly, I discuss what understanding peacekeeping as legitimized intervention means for the mission of UN peacekeeping, where peacekeeping is likely to be successful, and potential pathologies that may develop from states operating with a goal of protecting their own borders. More broadly, I consider what these interactions between the UN Security Council and other UN member states tell us about the consequences of institutional design for international organizations.

2

Conflict Externalities and the Incentive to Keep the Peace

THE UNITED NATIONS faces three dilemmas when seeking to form a new peacekeeping mission: (1) how to attract participants to the mission, (2) how to mobilize these contributors to deploy their personnel quickly, and (3) how to keep members committed to the mission throughout its duration. Each of these dilemmas stems from the underlying problem of collective action caused by the UN's institutional design. Because the UN does not have a standing military force, and it cannot compel its members to contribute troops, it must rely on its members to voluntarily provide peacekeeping personnel to a given mission. Furthermore, it must rely on those members to voluntarily keep their personnel committed to the mission. Observers generally point to two mechanisms that help the United Nations overcome these dilemmas. First, the UN can pay contributors for their personnel. This financial kickback may be enough incentive to motivate poorer states to lease their troops to the United Nations. Second, the UN's post–Cold War rhetoric has more fully embraced the goals of promoting human rights and protecting civilians through its peacekeeping missions. This shift in focus may help democratic states to participate for ideological reasons. Either the democracies see contributing to peacekeeping missions as in their interest to promote their norms abroad or they see peacekeeping as a lower-cost option to appease domestic humanitarian groups that urge the government to "do something" to help abused populations. Problematically, neither of these expectations suggests variance in the decision calculus of member states. Poor states participate whenever and wherever they can to capture monetary rents from their contributions. Democracies participate whenever and wherever they can to capture domestic ideological benefits from their contributions.

Member states, however, display wide variance in where they send their forces, when they become involved, and how long they remain committed to a given mission. Kenya, for example, has contributed to eighteen post–Cold War peacekeeping missions, but only three of them were outside Africa. Similar patterns exist for Senegal and Mali. Senegal has contributed to thirteen missions, and Mali has participated in nine. Neither country has ever deployed peacekeeping troops outside Africa. Although each of these countries has contributed significant personnel numbers to the UN's efforts, it is important to note that they each have also ignored the majority of the UN's calls for troops during this same period. Such patterns are troubling for previous explanations of peacekeeping participation because each of these countries is poor—standing at least a standard deviation below the global average gross domestic product per capita. Furthermore, Mali has been democratic for most of the post–Cold War period, and Kenya and Senegal have both been democracies for the latter half of this era. There is also significant variation in how quickly these countries have deployed their troops. Mali, for instance, participated immediately in the UN's Mission in Liberia, while waiting a year to contribute to UN efforts in Rwanda. Similarly, Senegal contributed immediately to the United Nations Operation in Côte d'Ivoire but waited over a year to participate in missions to the Democratic Republic of Congo (MONUC) and Rwanda. There is also significant variation in how long a state remains committed to a mission. For example, Kenya participated in the UN Mission in Sudan (UNMIS) for over six years, but it only contributed troops to the United Nations Mission in Burundi for two years.

In this chapter I present a theory to explain how the United Nations is able to overcome each of its dilemmas—attracting participants to missions quickly and keeping them committed long-term. Unlike previous explanations, this theory considers the direct connection between where a mission is deployed, how the conflict affects member states, and the benefits a member state might receive from helping to manage that specific conflict. Tying together these considerations, I am able to make precise predictions about where member states contribute, when they participate, and how long they stay involved with a given mission. Thus, this theory expects variation in decision-making and assesses outcomes in relation to this expected variation.

Refugee Flows and the Importance
of Stabilizing War Zones

Civil war causes a number of externalities for nearby states—such as weapons flows, porous borders, transborder rebel groups, declining trade, and food shortages. One of the most common concerns states face from nearby conflicts is the threat of refugee inflows. Refugees are individuals who have fled their home countries due to an inability to avail themselves of the protection of their government from abuse, conflict, or persecution. Since the 1960s, over 500 million individuals have become refugees (Marshall 2009). The situation in the post–Cold War era has not improved. At the end of 2017, unrest had produced 65.6 million forcibly displaced people worldwide, with conflicts in Syria, Afghanistan, and South Sudan producing the largest numbers of displaced persons. Over a third of these individuals have already crossed into another country as a refugee or asylum seeker, while the others remain internally displaced within their home country (UNHCR 2017). However, these internally displaced people remain a latent source of cross-border flows, and a growing concern for policymakers globally. For example, given domestic fear of social unrest and potential terrorist attacks, European policymakers have worked to keep Syrian refugees from entering Europe. They have developed an arrangement with Turkey whereby the European Union pays the Turkish government to host the refugees rather than letting them cross into European territory (*Guardian* 2017). Similarly, Israel has refused to allow Syrian refugees across its borders, fearing "a wave of illegal migrants and terrorist activities" (Stone 2016). Given these developments, the World Bank (2015) has recently emphasized research into "how to mitigate the potential negative socioeconomic impact of the refugee presence on host communities."

The reasons for these fears stem partially from the manner in which refugees may present myriad problems for the states to which they flee. Given their flight from conflict, refugees often lack shelter, clean drinking water, and nutritious food. These conditions expose the refugees to illnesses that spread easily in the migrants' tight, communal living conditions (Iqbal and Zorn 2010). Accommodating the refugees requires combating these health concerns, which can tax the state's health system, especially if the system needs to handle new diseases or viruses that it is not equipped to manage (Ghobarah, Huth, and Russett 2004). Similarly, the arrival of refugees stresses a state's food supply because refugees are more mouths to feed and may live off the land, creating shortages of harvestable food (Jenkins,

Scanlan, and Peterson 2007). In response to these concerns, the state must reallocate resources to survive these health and food strains. However, money diverted from the country's economic policies to addressing such problems can hurt the state's economy by diverting funds from investment and infrastructure, and slow the growth of gross domestic product (Murdoch and Sandler 2004). Such strains on the state's economy, food supplies, and health care often intertwine with xenophobic stances already present within a society, as the inflows may shift the country's demographics along ethnic or religious lines (Saideman and Ayres 2000). Together, these stresses help breed discontent and antagonism against the regime and threaten its survival.

Ignoring the potential turmoil created by the refugee inflows is problematic for the regime because these strains can bring civil war to the host country through two pathways. First, the strains detailed above can create grievances within the population. As individuals become dissatisfied with the state of the country's health care, economic performance, or food provision, they will seek ways to better their situation. Often, such dissatisfaction results in groups protesting or peacefully petitioning the government for change on its refugee policies, as many Germans did upon Chancellor Angela Merkel's initial welcoming of the Syrian refugees (*Guardian* 2017). In some cases, large-scale protests can result in a policy change or become destabilizing for the government on their own. However, if peacefully petitioning the government fails, some individuals become willing to turn to violence in an effort to force the government to address their grievances (Cederman and Vogt 2017), thus bringing civil conflict to the host country. Second, civil war, and thus refugee flows, tend to occur in "bad neighborhoods"—that is, conflicts and forced migration tend to cluster regionally (Weiner 1996). Part of the reason that conflicts cluster is the spreading of grievances, as just discussed. However, another reason that conflict tends to cluster is because refugee flows help the conflict to diffuse or become contagious. As forced migration occurs, strain is placed on the resources that states dedicate to securing their boarders. This allows more individuals to cross into and out of neighboring countries. Rebel fighters often hide among these flows of people, either preying on the vulnerable population or using the population as a place to hide before launching cross-border assaults (Salehyan and Gleditsch 2006). When the rebels enter the host country, they often use the violent tactics familiar to them to achieve their objectives in their new home, bringing civil war to the host state. For example, ex-FAR/Interahamwe fighters among the Hutu refugees in Zaire used violence to capture the town of Goma and begin Africa's World War (Salehyan 2008).

Given that ignoring the refugee inflows is not a feasible option, many governments take a stance that it is better to prevent further inflows and repatriate existing refugees than have to deal with the consequences of continued inflows. Therefore, as refugees enter the host state's territory and create the strains detailed above, the government will begin to look to stop further inflows. Stopping the inflows can take several forms, including closing borders, increasing a police presence along common cross-border passage points, or tightening airport security—all of which have been measures taken by governments to halt refugee inflows from Syria (Amnesty International 2014). However, a host government may believe that such domestic remedies may not be enough to halt inflows. Instead, the government may believe that the best way to decrease inflows is to address the foreign cause of the flows directly. When negotiating with the refugee-producing state, or funding humanitarian groups working with the refugees, fails, state-to-state responses may turn violent. Often, such conflict over refugee flows takes the form of military intervention (Regan 1998). The host state may intervene militarily into the ongoing civil war to end the hostilities that are creating the refugee flows. The idea behind such interventions is that if the host state can help end the conflict—either through military victory or negotiated settlement—then the refugee flows will end because there will no longer be a reason for individuals to flee their homes. For example, in 1971 the Bangladeshi war for independence from Pakistan created large refugee flows into India, with over 100,000 people crossing the broader each day (UNHCR 2000). When Pakistan refused to end the conflict and repatriate the displaced persons, India invaded the war zone to help the Bangladeshi rebels gain independence and end the war quickly (Salehyan 2008).

Although military intervention into the refugee-producing state may be appealing for the host state because it could end the inflows, such intervention into an ongoing civil war also possesses several potential problems. First, military intervention is costly. It requires mobilizing, supplying, and deploying the state's military. Given the turmoil at home, the intervening state may not have the resources to fully engage in the conflict. For example, Chad made a weak attempt to help the Democratic Republic of Congo (DRC) drive various rebel groups from its territory in 1998. However, without much domestic support for the action, and international condemnation of its troops' behavior, Chad withdrew its troops less than a year later without much success (Prunier 2009). Second, intervention in a civil war is often unsuccessful. Foreign parties tend to intervene when their preferred side is losing, making the war an uphill battle from the beginning of the intervention (Gent 2008). For instance, the Soviet invasion of Afghanistan began once the communist regime was nearing collapse (Gibbs 1987). The severity of fighting that ensues is often too much for the outside states, especially democratic states, which withdraw in the face of mounting casualties despite leaving the job unfinished (Wells 2016) and leaving the refugee crisis in place. Finally, military intervention can generate an international backlash. Intervening uninvited in the domestic affairs of another state is a violation of sovereignty and international norms. A state that violates the sovereignty of another is often named and shamed by other states and international organizations. Given these costs and risks, military action places the leader's political survival at risk (Bueno de Mesquita and Siverson 1995). Domestic constituents do not like casualties, and they do not like losing. Unsuccessful intervention thus threatens the leader's postconflict tenure, especially if the refugee inflows have not abated. States receiving refugee inflows thus face a dilemma. How can they help reduce the refugee inflows they face while minimizing the costs and risk of their involvement?

Peacekeeping as Refugee Reduction

Peacekeeping offers an alternative approach to unilateral military intervention for states interested in helping end a conflict. Peacekeeping is a conflict-management strategy in which countries from outside the wartorn country—what are called "third parties" because they are not an initial party to the conflict—enter the conflict zone with troops tasked to keep the parties from fighting as they attempt to peacefully negotiate an end to the conflict. Peacekeeping is conducted by individual states (e.g., Nigeria, in the DRC, 1964–65) and regional organizations (e.g., the Economic Community of West African States, in Liberia, 1990–99); however, the United Nations is the primary peacekeeping entity (e.g., UNMISS, in South Sudan, 2011–present). Interestingly, peacekeeping was not a function developed in the initial design of the organization. Instead, the UN's role in peacekeeping developed out of its duties under Chapter VI of the UN Charter to help settle disputes between its members peacefully and its Chapter VII duties of taking action to address threats to international peace and security. Thus, peacekeeping is sometimes referred to as a

Chapter VI-½ function. Nonetheless, as peacekeeping has become a significant tool of the United Nations, the organization has developed three basic principles to guide its peacekeeping missions: (1) gaining consent of the conflictual parties, (2) being impartial in its treatment of the factions, and (3) not using military force except in self-defense. Gaining consent is meant to help in the political process of ending the conflict because the parties have signaled their interest in having outside help to resolve the issue in dispute. Impartiality is designed to keep the parties cooperating with the organization and each other, in hopes that neither feels like the target of the international community. Finally, the lack of force is also meant to signal to the belligerents that dialogue is the best way to resolve the conflict. In some instances, however, the United Nations will authorize a peacekeeping or "peace enforcement" operation under Chapter VII of the UN Charter and authorize peacekeepers to use any force necessary when it determines there is no functioning government (e.g., Somalia) or the situation is a grave threat to civilians (e.g., Mali) (Durall 2013).

The question arises of how the United Nations can effectively help end conflict and reduce refugee flows if it is often unwilling to use force or to take a side in the conflict. Setting aside the important diplomatic portion of peacekeeping that is dedicated to ending the conflict and developing a lasting peace, I focus on the role of peacekeepers in country to outline how peacekeeping provides an alternative mechanism for host states to help reduce the refugee inflows they experience. Peacekeeping troops undertake three types of actions that help contribute to reducing refugee flows from the conflict country (Hultman, Kathman, and Shannon 2013 also tie these actions to civilian protection more generally). The first type of action in which peacekeepers engage is helping to separate the warring factions from each other. Keeping the combatants separate requires establishing a clear cease-fire line, patrolling the line for violations, and monitoring combatant behavior to establish early warnings of potential purposeful or accidental cease-fire violations. These activities are helpful in reducing refugee flows, for two main reasons. First, when the belligerents are separated, they are unlikely to fight one another. With a decreased threat of military violence, civilians within the war zone will be less tempted to leave the area for fear of becoming collateral damage from the conflict. Second, when the parties are separated, they have less access to each other's civilian populations. Without access to these populations, they are unlikely to target their enemies' support population in hopes of killing potential fighters or breaking the morale of the people. Without fear of being targeted by the enemy, civilians in the area are also less likely to flee across borders looking for protection.

The second action that peacekeepers take is separating a warring party from its support population, or the group it claims to represent. Separating the group from the population is important because while some civilians willingly support the cause, others are coerced into providing money, food, or shelter to the group. The peacekeepers police interactions between fighters and civilians, making sure that the fighters are not abusing or coercing the population. This police protection helps members of the community feel safer at home, decreasing the probability that they will leave to become refugees. If they are not being forced to support the rebels, they will have more resources to reestablish their lives after the conflict. Finally, peacekeepers directly work to support the local population by delivering food, empowering women, and protecting children. Along with these direct activities, peacekeepers also bring with them civilian experts that can advise on and help with programs designed specifically to demobilize child soldiers and stop the use of sexual violence (see DPKO 2018h). Each of these activities helps protect the population, increases the civilians' standard of living, and provides some insurance that remaining at home is a feasible choice. As with the first two activities, the peacekeeper's focus on providing goods, services, and safety to the civilian population helps reduce the factors that push individuals out of their home countries and into a neighboring country as refugees (see Moore and Shellman 2004). Thus, these peacekeeping activities help reduce the refugee outflows from the war-torn country and, in turn, the inflows arriving in the host countries (Beardsley 2011).

Not only can peacekeepers help protect civilians in the ways just discussed, but such protection has also become central to the design and implementation of the UN's peacekeeping missions. After the UN's failure to protect civilians in the former Yugoslavia, Rwanda, and Somalia during the early 1990s, the UN's Department of Peacekeeping Operations (DPKO) reassessed how best to resolve conflicts and how to better protect civilians so that such failures do not happen again. Since this period of self-reflection, the Security Council and DPKO have worked to make civilian protection the cornerstone of the UN's peacekeeping efforts. These developments have resulted in the Security Council crafting its mandates, and its resolutions on the conflicts in which it becomes involved, in the context of civilian protection. Today, more than 95 percent of UN peacekeepers are mandated to protect civilians (DPKO 2018f). According to the High-Level

Independent Panel on Peace Operations (HIPPO 2015), civilian protection should continue to be at the core of the UN's obligations to create greater international peace and stability. This means there is unlikely to be a shift away from this focus on protecting civilians in the near future. Instead, the tools that the UN uses to help protect civilians through its peacekeeping missions are likely to be strengthened and further expanded, as the Security Council finds civilian protection to be of utmost importance to successfully ending conflict. Thus, peacekeeping is likely to remain a vehicle through which third parties can help reduce refugee inflows into their territory.

Peacekeeping through the United Nations also helps lower the costs and risks for third parties seeking to become involved in managing the humanitarian crisis caused by the conflict. First, the United Nations reimburses contributors roughly $1,400 per troop per month that they contribute. This reimbursement is paid directly to the government and helps offset any military expenses that the state may have incurred in outfitting the peacekeeping troops. Additionally, assessments are imposed on all UN member states to help pay for the peacekeeping mission, so that each contributor state does not have to bear the auxiliary costs associated with sending troops abroad. Together, the monetary reimbursement and the offsetting of deployment costs help lower the financial costs associated with entering the war-torn country for the third party relative to what it would need to pay to conduct a similar intervention unilaterally (DPKO 2014). Second, the operation's required personnel levels are split across the contributing countries. This means that each contributor bears a much lower military burden than it would need to shoulder if it were to intervene unilaterally in the country. Thus, the costs and the risks associated with the mission are mitigated by exposing more governments to these costs. Third, unlike in many unilateral state interventions, the United Nations attempts to work with both sides of the conflict before deploying troops. By laying the groundwork for a successful operation before troops are deployed, the UN lowers the probability that the mission will fail. Using its political clout and its dedication to continuing communication with each side in the conflict, the UN sees a high rate of success in its peacekeeping efforts (DPKO 2014). This high likelihood of success decreases a leader's fear of postinvolvement punishment for an unsuccessful mission. Additionally, the leader can use the United Nations as a scapegoat if anything goes wrong in the mission. Finally, the United Nations possesses a legitimacy for peacekeeping that individual states do not possess (Boutros-Ghali 1999). Working through the United Nations provides states cover for the work they do within the borders of another country, reducing backlash for crossing international borders.

Overall, then, states desire to stop refugee inflows because of the domestic strains they create. When domestic remedies to stopping inflows—such as tighter border security—do not work and peaceful negotiations with the refugees' home state fail, a state becomes more willing to use force against the refugees' home state to accomplish its goals of ending inflows. However, intervening in a civil war is both costly and risky when done unilaterally. The United Nations' peacekeeping efforts provide an avenue for concerned states to intervene abroad, while lowering the potential costs and risks associated with such an operation. The in-country actions of peacekeepers help reduce the conditions that push civilian populations out of their homes and across international borders as refugees. Therefore, peacekeeping can provide benefits to its participants directly related to the conflict being managed through the operation. Because peacekeepers can help stabilize a war-torn area, and reduce the number of refugees leaving the area, contributing to a successful peacekeeping mission benefits a state by lowering the externalities it may receive from the conflict, and by helping reduce the likelihood that it will be drawn into a nearby conflict. A state's desire to contribute peacekeeping troops should thus be linked to the benefits it receives from securing its borders. Note that this argument is different from one that focuses on the total number of displaced persons fleeing a conflict. Rather than focusing on forced migration as a global humanitarian concern (e.g., Bove and Elia 2011), this argument suggests that direct dyadic flows from the conflict country to a third-party state help explain the third party's willingness to contribute to the peacekeeping mission.

Refugees and the UN's Peacekeeping Contribution Dilemmas

The United Nations has refocused its peacekeeping efforts on protecting civilians. These operations now provide a direct means for helping reduce refugee outflows from the war-torn country. Indeed, in his 2007 report on the protection of civilians in armed conflict, UN Secretary-General Ban Ki-moon (2007) directly connected the protection of civilians to the ability to halt forced migration. The question remains, however, how the incentive to reduce refugee inflows connects to the UN's three dilemmas in how to attract participants to missions, how to mobilize those contributors to deploy their personnel quickly, and how to keep members committed to the mission throughout its duration. In answering this question, it is important to note that member states do not contribute their soldiers to a general peacekeeping pool that the UN can use to distribute personnel across its ongoing missions. Instead, members are able to contribute their military personnel to specific conflicts. For instance, Ethiopia has chosen to contribute soldiers, and it ranks in the top five contributing states, to the ongoing African Union–United Nations Hybrid Operation in Darfur, Sudan, in South Sudan (United Nations Mission in South Sudan, UNMISS), and in the disputed territory between Sudan and South Sudan (United Nations Interim Security Force for Abyei); but it has contributed no, or very few, peacekeepers to the UN's other eleven ongoing missions (DPKO 2018a). This design of the institution means that a member state can make strategic decisions about where and when to send its troops. Therefore, in resolving the puzzle around the UN's three peacekeeping dilemmas, it is important to also answer the question of where each participating member is contributing its personnel. For example, why does Ethiopia send troops to Sudan and South Sudan but not to the Central African Republic? To understand these choices, I posit that observers of peacekeeping contributions must take into account features of the mission and how the conflict affects individual UN members. That is, we need to consider conflict- and mission-specific factors to understand member behavior.

Refugee inflows are the crucial aspect of each conflict that I expect to help drive member behavior in each given mission. Although refugee outflows may be considered global humanitarian crises, especially as the size of the outflows increases, refugees tend to cluster in countries near their own. For example, in 2014, at the beginning of its civil war, South Sudan produced over 600,000 refugees. Yet only four states received more than 10,000 of these refugees (UNHCR 2018). Therefore, even large humanitarian crises tend to affect states disproportionately, with some states experiencing the costs of the conflict to a greater degree than others. Given these dynamics, I do not expect total refugee outflows from a country, and thus the overall severity of the humanitarian crisis, to influence member states' behavior as much as the magnitude to which the crisis affects each state individually. Given the threat a state faces from refugee inflows, it should be more likely than other countries to work to provide peace and security and to protect the at-risk population in that specific conflict zone so that the refugees do not continue to enter its territory. If the state can eliminate the source of the refugee problem, then it will be better off for not having to face the tensions created by these arrivals as they continue to enter the country. It is due to the fear of the consequences of these inflows that many states are willing to take efforts abroad to stabilize war-torn countries and protect civilians in the area.

This is not to say that states which are receiving no or low numbers of refugees from a conflict will not participate in a mission. For example, Nepal and Bangladesh both contribute peacekeepers broadly. However, a state must be strategic in how it distributes its military personnel. A state is unlikely to dedicate personnel to situations in which it will receive little or no return on its investment. Resources dedicated to low-return projects are wasteful for the state because it no longer has these goods at its service and it has not fortified its position. In terms of dispatching peacekeeping troops, this implies that a state will be unlikely to participate in operations that will not have an effect on preventing refugees from entering its territory. Troops sent to areas that are unlikely to produce refugees for the state cannot help the state achieve its goal of stopping inflows. To help clarify this logic, consider the situation of Ethiopia, in which it chooses between contributing to the UN's peacekeeping mission in South Sudan (UNMISS) or to the UN mission in the Central African Republic (MINUSCA), noting that both South Sudan and the Central African Republic (CAR) are within Ethiopia's region. Note that both South Sudan and the CAR are facing large humanitarian crises, given the ongoing civil wars in these two counties. However, only the conflict in South Sudan has produced refugee inflows for Ethiopia, despite both conflicts having produced nearly a million forced migrants since 2011. If Ethiopia contributes troops to MINUSCA, these soldiers will be able to help ameliorate the humanitarian crisis in the CAR, but they will be unable to alleviate the violence that is driving the refugees into Ethiopia. Though these troops may limit violence in the CAR, from Ethiopia's point of view and given its concerns, these personnel are not used in a beneficial manner, because they do not help Ethiopia stem the tide of refugees entering its territory from South Sudan.

With the particular problem of preventing refugee inflows as motivation, and a strategy of directing its personnel toward relieving this problem, a state expecting refugee inflows from a specific conflict will focus its forces on the actual area of concern rather than another conflict. This helps explain Ethiopia's current involvement in UNMISS and its absence from MINUSCA. It also helps explain why this poor state does not contribute broadly and why this nondemocracy is interested in helping protect civilian populations. Also, consider the United States. Unlike Ethiopia, the United States is a wealthy democracy. Similar to Ethiopia, however, the United States rarely contributes troops to UN peacekeeping missions. However, there have been a few key exceptions. Primarily, as part of the United Nations Mission in Haiti (UNMIH), the United States contributed over 2,000 yearly troops to missions in Haiti after experiencing nearly 7,000 refugees from the small island country before joining this mission. Following this logic,

Hypothesis 1: A state is more likely to contribute to peacekeeping missions in situations from which it is experiencing refugee inflows.

In addition to influencing the likelihood of participation, refugee inflows should also affect the size of a state's contribution. Conflicts producing higher levels of refugees are more destabilizing to the region and require stronger third-party action to help end the conflict (e.g., Fortna 2008). A state interested in ending refugee outflows from the target country must consider the force size necessary to successfully stabilize the conflict country and stem the refugee flows it is receiving. Holding costs of participation constant, as the conflict produces more refugee inflows for a state, the state is likely to scale up its contribution in relation. Severe conflicts that produce a large number of refugee outflows will require more third-party troops to keep the peace and prevent the violence that causes refugee outflows (e.g., Hultman, Kathman, and Shannon 2013). Therefore, as a state receives more refugees from a particular conflict, the state is likely to contribute more troops to the peacekeeping mission that is dedicated to that war-torn country because it feels pressure to dedicate the additional force needed to stem the flows more quickly in these situations than when it is receiving few externalities. Consider Ethiopia again. Between its involvement in Sudan and South Sudan, Ethiopia is contributing to three ongoing UN peacekeeping missions. The African Union–United Nations Hybrid Operation in Darfur, Sudan, produced few refugees for Ethiopia. Conversely, the United Nations Interim Security Force for Abyei and UMISS are located in or on the border of South Sudan, which has produced over 330,000 refugees for Ethiopia. In line with the logic I have provided, Ethiopia is currently providing 140 percent more troops to the South Sudanese missions than to the one in Darfur, despite being the largest contributor of peacekeeping personnel in Darfur (DPKO 2018a):

Hypothesis 2: A state is likely to contribute more troops to peacekeeping missions in situations from which it is experiencing higher volumes of refugee inflows.

Consider this logic in the context of the United States' role in creating and conducting the UNMIH. In 1991, Jean-Bertrand Aristide took office as the democratically elected president of Haiti. Seven months later, the Haitian military overthrew Aristide under the direction of Lieutenant-General Raoul Cédras. Cédras's junta was brutal and created a mass exodus of Haitian refugees that predominantly arrived in the Dominican Republic and the United States (UNHCR 2018). These outflows moved the situation in Haiti to the top of the United States' foreign policy concerns, as the United States maneuvered in the Organization of American States (OAS) to find a solution to the crisis (Kreps 2007). Despite diplomatic efforts and an economic embargo by the OAS throughout 1991 and 1992, Cédras refused to relinquish control of Haiti. The refugee flows continued, and refugee policy became a debate point during the 1992 US presidential election (Girard 2004). By November 1992, the UN General Assembly adopted a resolution that demanded the restoration of the Aristide regime and requested the UN secretary-general to take the necessary measures in order to assist in the Haitian crisis. Aristide also asked the secretary-general to deploy a mission of civilians to monitor the situation in Haiti (DPKO 2018c).

By 1993, the United States was receiving half of all refugees fleeing Haiti (UNHCR 2018). These inflows intensified domestic debate in the United States concerning how to handle the Haitian crisis. Military officials saw the refugee situation as a security concern, and members of Congress were being pressured by their constituents to stop the inflows. In response, US President Bill Clinton adamantly announced that "the simple fact is that we must not—and will not—surrender our borders to those who wish to exploit our history of compassion and justice," as he intensified the United States' repatriation efforts (Girard 2004, 56). This policy proved divisive domestically, and Clinton began to pressure the UN to take more decisive action in Haiti. US pressure was effective. In April 1993, the UN authorized the Civilian Mission in Haiti in conjunction with the OAS, and by June Aristide and Cédras agreed to a dialogue with UN support. The Security Council then authorized UNMIH in September 1993. However, when UNMIH personnel attempted to land in Haiti, militia loyal to Cédras refused to allow them to enter the country. Furthermore, Cédras's forces prevented Aristide from returning to the island. With diplomatic efforts halted, violence escalating, and UNMIH stalled, the observers from the Civilian Mission in Haiti were withdrawn.

Throughout the remainder of 1993 and into 1994, the United Nations and the OAS increased sanctions on the Cédras regime, to no avail. However, sensitive to how the sanctions could push additional Haitians into fleeing the country, the United States excluded basic food staples and cooking oil from the economic embargo (Girard 2004, 56). The United States then deployed additional naval vessels to better quarantine Haiti and increase pressure on Cédras. But the situation in Haiti continued to deteriorate. In response, US military officials began to assess the political and military feasibility of invading Haiti and concluded that conditions were favorable. US military planners developed a strategy whereby the United States alone would handle the predeployment and initial deployment of military forces into Haiti before then leading multilateral forces in country with UN authorization (Kreps 2007, 460). However, domestic and international observers argued that the United States should take a more international approach to the situation, and in July 1994, the United States solicited token support from other countries. By the end of the month, the UN Security Council established a multinational force (MNF) to assist in the US-led Operation Restore Democracy, authorizing the mission to "use all necessary means to facilitate the departure from Haiti of the military leadership."

With forces ready to deploy, President Clinton continued to build domestic US political support for the operation. The message from the president and his supporters continued to focus on the refugee situation. In defending his decision to intervene, Clinton directly referenced the need to halt the conflict to stop refugee flows due to the costs they were imposing on America: "We have a particular interest in stopping brutality when it occurs so close to our shores. . . . As long as Cédras rules, Haitians will continue to seek sanctuary in our nation. This year, in less than two months, more than 21,000 Haitians were rescued at sea by our Coast Guard and Navy. Today more than 14,000 refugees are living at our naval base in Guantánamo. The American people have already spent $177 million to support them" (White House 1994). Admiral Paul Miller used similar language in selling the invasion: "Nine million Haitians off our shores—and they all want to be your neighbors" (Girard 2004, 56).

In September 1994, the MNF deployed with US troops accounting for over 97 percent of the soldiers landing in Haiti. US troops then secured key strategic sites and instructed the non-US soldiers to conduct security operations in the peripheral Haitian cities (Kreps 2007). The US military remained in control as power transitioned back to Aristide, and not until January 1995 did UNMIH personnel begin to redeploy to Haiti. Even then, the United States only relinquished peacekeeping responsibilities to UNMIH on March 31, 1995. Furthermore, though formal responsibility now rested with the United Nations, the United States remained the primary contributor of military personnel to UNMIH until the mission concluded in 1996 and commanded the military component of UNMIH. This was the first time the United States commanded a UN peacekeeping operation (Ramalho and Neto 2015). The United States also monitored the 1995 Haitian election, trained the Haitian police force, and provided funds for small development projects in the country. Such behavior stands in contrast with the United States' general approach to UN peacekeeping, which is to fund the missions without contributing troops (DPKO 2014). Making this participation even more astonishing was that it occurred in the aftermath of the United States' failure in Somalia and the Black Hawk Down incident that had instituted a more conservative approach to US involvement in UN operations (Ramalho and Neto 2015). However, as Girard (2004, 56) states, "The fear of a Haitian exodus shaped US policies in Haiti" and also influenced its subsequent involvement in both Operation Restore Democracy and UNMIH.

A second key feature of UN peacekeeping missions is that they allow states to contribute or withdraw personnel throughout the duration of the mission. Although some states contribute early in the operation, others wait before participating. For example, while Kenya contributed troops to the United Nations Mission in Ethiopia and Eritrea at the beginning of the operation, Algeria and Uruguay waited nearly three years to participate. Similarly, Kenya contributed troops to UNMIS at the mission's beginning, while Brazil, Japan, and Sierra Leone each waited over three years to participate. These institutional rules to peacekeeping contributions mean that the decision about peacekeeping contribution is a dynamic process rather than a static choice. The conflict-specific approach I offer for understanding peacekeeping contributions posits that both the timing of when states contribute and withdraw personnel from a particular peace operation is determined, in part, by the evolutionary nature of conflicts and their effects on the member states. Two conditions influence the timing of participation. First, the benefits of intervention need to outweigh the costs (e.g., Gent 2008). As discussed above, there are many costs, and thus potential obstacles, to both military intervention and peacekeeping. Therefore, third parties are hesitant to send their troops into another country's domestic turmoil. However, the dynamics of the civil war may provide benefits to intervention, as they produce refugee outflows to influence member participation in the war-torn country. The issue, however, is that refugee outflows fluctuate throughout the course of the conflict. These flows tend to fluctuate in relation to the variability of three conflict-specific factors. First, fighting that occurs near more heavily populated areas is likely to produce more outflows than fighting in other areas because more individuals are affected by the violence. Second, more severe fighting is likely to produce more outflows because the violence both likely affects more people and creates a greater source of fear for those individuals. Finally, when parties in the conflict resort to targeting civilians directly, the level of refugee outflows increases because now members of the population know that they are likely targets of the violence if they do not flee (Uzonyi 2014).

Changing strategic incentives are crucial to understanding the timing of contributions because the second condition necessary for third-party involvement is that the benefits of participation appear pressing to the third party. Even if contributing may appear beneficial to a member, the state may not participate if it does not perceive a need to obtain those benefits quickly. It is once the benefits of participation outweigh the costs of action and the member perceives capturing these benefits as pressing that intervention takes place (Findley and Teo 2006). If the need for intervention does not appear pressing, then a third party may be willing to postpone intervention to obtain more information about the situation from other involved states (Balch-Lindsay and Enterline 2000). This is one of the primary obstacles to humanitarian endeavors such as peacekeeping. Even if members of the international community see benefit in intervening in a conflict, they may believe it is best to allow others to act first rather than commit their personnel on pursuing the benefits of stabilizing a war-torn country (Gent 2007). Thus, nearby conflict or low numbers of refugee inflows may not be enough to promote participation by a given member state.

However, the desire to prevent continued refugee inflows from a conflict can help third-party states overcome the collective action problem and respond quickly to the UN's call for help. Given its desire to prevent the problems associated with refugee inflows, a state receiving spillovers from a conflict area will need to act swiftly. Once refugees enter a country, it is difficult to remove them (Loescher and Milner 2005). This is evident from the length of time refugee camps tend to endure in their host countries. For example, the Dadaab Camp established in Kenya during 1992 for refugees from the Somali civil war is still in place today. This camp appears to have developed into a semipermanent destination for refugees, as thousands of individuals flee to the shelter yearly (UNHCR 2012). Attacking refugees in an attempt to drive them out will bring scorn from nongovernmental organizations and other leaders, and it is a crime against humanity (International Criminal Court 2011). This limits the state's options for removing the refugees. Furthermore, rushing refugees through the asylum process costs the state money, labor, and time. Once an individual's asylum appeal has been rejected, the state must dedicate further resources to deport the refugee. To avoid these logistical issues, and the tensions it fears, a state experiencing refugee inflows should work quickly to alleviate the foreign situation that is causing these externalities. Therefore, it should be these states experiencing refugee inflows from the target country that contribute troops most quickly to a peacekeeping mission in the target country.

It is important to note that the urgency of intervention for a state evolves over the course of a conflict as the civil war situation changes. This urgency maps onto the rate of refugee flows into the country. As the location, severity, and tactics of the war change, the urgency of the situation fluctuates for each of the UN's member states. Some countries will not receive refugees from the conflict country until later in the civil war or peacekeeping operation. Without the threat of the turmoil that increasing refugee inflows create for a state, those countries without significant initial inflows will not perceive an urgency to participate until the externalities of the conflict begin to mount for them. Ghana, for example, did not receive annual inflows of over 600 refugees from Sudan until 2006 (UNHCR 2018) and waited until then to contribute troops to UNMIS (DPKO 2018a). Considering peacekeeping as a method of externality prevention for specific conflicts thus also helps explain late contributors:

Hypothesis 3: A state is likely to commit troops more quickly to peacekeeping missions in situations from which it is experiencing higher volumes of refugee inflows.

Note that this is an instrumental view of peacekeeping. States use peacekeeping to accomplish specific foreign policy goals. In particular, they use the blue helmet of UN peacekeeping as a legitimizing cover to effect domestic change in another state (Gibbs 1997). This is a dyadic argument. Each time a peacekeeping mission is authorized, the member states consider whether participation in that mission will be advantageous to their goals.

The member states make this determination based on the consequences they face from each given mission, not necessarily the international situation. The state is concerned with the refugees it directly faces from that specific conflict, not the global humanitarian crisis the conflict may create more broadly.

The dyadic logic I propose means that a contributing state has certain expectations about what it hopes to accomplish by working through the UN apparatus. Helping to protect the at-risk population by providing peacekeepers should result in lower flows of refugees to the contributing state. Although UN peacekeeping missions often succeed in reducing externality flows and stabilizing regions (Beardsley 2011), failures do occur (e.g., MONUC). If working through the United Nations fails to stem the refugees the state experiences once joining the mission, a state will update its expectations about the value of participating in the operation. In situations where the state continues to experience refugee flows from the managed conflict, it will likely look for options outside the United Nations to accomplish its goals.

Committing troops to a UN mission generates "sunk" political and military costs for a member state's government. Political costs are related to the government's spending of political capital to convince its constituents that the mission is worth supporting. For instance, political costs could include calling in favors or placing one's reputation on the line. Military costs are related to deploying troops and reducing one's preparedness for preventing domestic or international conflict. For instance, military costs can include deployment salaries, risking the destruction of equipment, or not having units near home for defense. These political and military concerns are costs the government incurs for deploying troops and committing military resources to the mission that it cannot recover (Fearon 1997). Withdrawing early from the mission may lead to additional domestic political costs, as constituents and opponents question the government's competency for deploying troops to a failed mission (e.g., Smith 1998).

However, remaining committed to an operation while the mission is failing to deliver its expected value also generates domestic costs. Here, not only do constituents and opponents question the government's competency for deploying troops to a failed mission, but they can also question why the regime is not taking steps to remedy the growing problems created by the refugee inflows. I argue that leaders compare their sunk and potential withdraw costs with their expected future costs for remaining committed to the mission. When the expected future costs appear to outweigh sunk costs, the government withdraws from the mission. However, this requires the government to overcome the sunk cost fallacy (see Arkes and Blumer 1985) and the fear of policy reversal. Some regimes may be more likely to deviate from a failing policy than others. For example, democracies (which fear long deployments) and wealthier states (which have more policy options) are most sensitive to continued refugee levels and may be most willing to withdraw, given continued high inflows. Although such variation is likely, and can be explored empirically, the simplest and most conservative proposition from this argument is that a state is likely to withdraw more quickly from a peacekeeping mission in situations where it continues to receive higher volumes of refugee inflows, despite the peacekeepers' presence:[1]

> Hypothesis 4: A state is likely to withdraw more quickly from a peacekeeping mission in situations where it continues to receive higher volumes of refugee inflows, despite the peacekeepers' presence.

The case of UNMIH illustrates these two hypotheses well. Each country receiving over 1,000 refugees from Haiti in 1995 after the MNF relinquished control of the mission to UNMIH participated in the peacekeeping operation as soon as it resumed. Furthermore, the mission was successful in reducing refugee flows. All these host countries, other than the United States, saw their inflows decrease over the duration of UNMIH and remained committed to the mission until its conclusion. The United States initially saw its inflows increase slightly. However, given that the United States controlled both the MNF and UNMIH under the legitimizing banner of the United Nations (Kreps 2007), it saw continuing to operate through these channels as its best alternative in handling inflows from Haiti. Furthermore, within two years, inflows to the United States began to decline. Therefore, though the dynamics of UNMIH speak well to my theory, the United States' overwhelming influence in this operation, and its ability to quickly and soundly defeat Cédras's forces, may not make UNMIH an ideal case through which to fully evaluate the dynamics posited in Hypothesis 4.

Consider, instead, Tanzania's involvement in MONUC, its early withdrawal from the operation, and its return to the DRC as part of the UN's Force Intervention Brigade. In July 1999, participants in Africa's World War signed the Lusaka Agreement, noted the refugee crises caused by the conflict, and requested peacekeeping assistance from the United Nations. On November 30, the Security Council authorized MONUC with specific focus on stopping refugee outflows from the DRC and repatriating those refugees that had already left the country. Tanzania was intimately involved in this process because it was part of the Southern African Development Community's (SADC) mediation effort in the DRC that helped realize the cease-fire. Tanzania had also received over 150,000 refugees from the DRC between 1998 and 1999 (Cilliers and Malan 2001). However, Tanzania was hesitant to join MONUC, believing that stabilizing the Great Lakes Region should be an African enterprise. And MONUC was struggling. Only three months after its initial mandate, the Security Council authorized phase II of MONUC, noting its trouble handling the refugee situation. Despite the renewed efforts, the refugee problem continued, and SADC accused the UN of being overcautious (Security Council 2000).

Tanzania was one of the states critical of the UN effort. In the year since MONUC was founded, Tanzania had received over 11,000 refugees from the DRC. In January 2001, Tanzania joined MONUC as SADC urged for increasing military involvement in the DRC. But the UN's increasing presence in the DRC did little to solve the refugee problem. Violations of the Lusaka Agreement were frequent, with open combat occurring along the DRC's borders with Burundi and Tanzania. This fighting intensified the refugee crisis for Tanzania as it continued to receive refugees from both the DRC and Burundi. In 2001 alone, Tanzania hosted over 500,000 refugees from Burundi. These inflows created tensions between Burundi and Tanzania as several rebel groups also crossed their border, recruiting among the refugees, and attacking Burundi from Tanzania (Integrated Regional Information Network 2001). The United Nations considered extending MONUC's mandate to cover Tanzania in hopes of better addressing Tanzania's concerns, but Tanzania had had enough. By April, only three months after its initial contributions, Tanzania withdrew from MONUC. Tanzania then took military action, moving its troops into position along the border with Burundi, and it began forcing refugees back into Burundi (Security Council 2001).

To help end the refugee inflows it was receiving, Tanzania joined the United Nations Mission in the Democratic Republic of Congo. However, when the operation failed to help Tanzania achieve its foreign policy goals, it withdrew from the mission to handle the situation on its own terms, using methods of which the UN disproved. For over a decade, Tanzania operated outside the auspices of the UN. However, in 2013, with its civil wars continuing, the DRC invited several of its neighbors, including Tanzania, to intervene militarily in the conflict to end the fighting. This was an invitation for war rather than peacekeeping. Concerned that such intervention would interfere with its reinvented presence in the DRC (now named the United Nations Organization Stabilization Mission in the Democratic Republic of the Congo), the United Nations asked these neighbors to operate their forces as part of its peace enforcement efforts. In response, Tanzania led the formation of the Force Intervention Bridge (FIB) alongside Malawi and South Africa. As the United States had done with the MNF, Tanzania treated the FIB as its own military intervention. Its mandate for action came from the DRC, not the Security Council. This approach of disguising its military intervention as a UN mission has led Tanzania and its allies to disregard the UN's rules of engagement. Despite its ties to the UN, the FIB has been brutal in its campaign to finally defeat the rebels in the DRC. These tactics and the FIB's independence from the UN's efforts have led observers to note that the FIB is realistically an independent geopolitical balancing effort by these states rather than a UN peacekeeping force (Minde 2016; Moloo 2016). As of 2019, the FIB is still engaged in what appears to be open warfare within the DRC under the legitimacy of the United Nations. Refugee inflows remain a concern; but in this incarnation of MONUC, Tanzania has more control over achieving its foreign policy goals. Leaving MONUC when it became dissatisfied with the mission's level of success thus provided Tanzania with other avenues through which to pursue its goals of ending the refugee inflows it was receiving from the DRC.

Summary

In this chapter, I have presented a theory of member state involvement in United Nations peacekeeping operations that is based on conflict- and mission-specific considerations. I posit that mission-specific concerns about direct externalities from the conflict help shape a member's willingness to participate in a mission. Specifically, states receiving refugee inflows from the target country are more likely to participate, participate quickly, and contribute a greater number of soldiers to the peacekeeping mission. However, participating in the mission also shapes the member state's expectations about the size of future inflows from the conflict. If the peacekeeping operation is unable to decrease the inflows of refugees the state is experiencing from the target country, then the member is likely to withdraw from the mission sooner than states not receiving inflows. Therefore, though refugee flows help the United Nations overcome its first two dilemmas in establishing a peacekeeping mission, they can also undermine the

UN's efforts in solving its third dilemma of keeping states committed to the operation. Paradoxically, when the mission falters, it is those states with the least stake in solving the crisis that are most likely to remain committed to the operation. In the next chapter, I test these propositions econometrically to analyze whether my theory receives support in situations across time and space beyond the case studies I have presented here.

Note

1. A state's decision to withdraw early from a mission is different from the case when the UN winds down a mission and a state's services are no longer required—for example, when the Bahamas left UNMIH one month before the Security Council fully transitioned the mission.

3

Analyzing the Argument

I HAVE ARGUED that conflict and mission-specific member state interests, rather than member-specific characteristics (e.g., democracy or poverty), help the United Nations overcome the dilemmas of recruiting peacekeeping participants and motivating participants to contribute to the operation early. Specifically, I focus on refugee inflows as a primary concern of member states. Those states receiving inflows from war-torn countries look for a method to prevent additional inflows and repatriate the refugees they have received in order to avoid domestic turmoil and conflict from the influx of forced migrants. Peacekeeping provides a lower-cost option to solving this problem because it reduces the violent factors that push individuals out of their home country and into host countries. Refugee host states value this tool because the UN legitimizes their presence in the refugees' home country and provides them a method to stop additional inflows. In the post–Cold War era, where the United Nations emphasizes civilian protection, peacekeeping provides a natural bridge between the domestic and foreign policy concerns of its member states in stopping refugee inflows and the organization's interest in protecting human rights in war zones. From this argument, I develop four observable implications. I test each of these hypotheses econometrically in this section. The models presented in this chapter provide strong support for Hypotheses 1, 3, and 4. Overall, they support my specific claim that refugee flows help shape a member state's willingness to contribute to specific UN peacekeeping missions. They also support my broader claim that conflict- and mission-specific factors tend to outweigh the member-specific factors on which previous research has focused.

I also consider these patterns in the case of the United Nations Mission in Sudan (UNMIS). UNMIS was a complex mission, whose mandate included specific language focusing on the protection of civilians and the repatriation of refugees. Despite unanimous support from the Security Council, however, UNMIS was slow to attract participation, and its contributors never provided enough troops to satisfy the mission's mandate (Hansen 2015). The participation patterns throughout this mission support my claims that refugee inflows greatly shape how states respond to the UN's calls for action. This case also illustrates some of the other patterns revealed by the econometric analysis, reinforcing Bellamy and Williams's (2013) claim that no one factor drives all peacekeeping contributions. However, refugee flows tend to explain significant patterns across different peacekeeping behaviors, while other factors do not.

Similarly, I consider the case of the United Nations Multidimensional Integrated Stabilization Mission in Mali (MINUSMA), which is one of the United Nations' newest peacekeeping missions. Like UNMIS, MINUSMA has remained understaffed since its formation. Refugee flows greatly shaped which states contributed to the mission. However, the United Nations' partnership with the African Union (AU) and Economic Community of West African States (ECOWAS) has helped it overcome issues with early withdrawal, as ECOWAS has used its institutionalized Standby Force to motivate continued participation in the mission. The patterns revealed through this case study highlight the importance of institutional design and some of the advantages and disadvantages the United Nations faces when partnering with regional organizations to field a peacekeeping operation.

Research Design

The theory I present in chapter 2 produces four observable implications. Each of these implications is a testable hypothesis of the theory, and each hypothesis needs to be tested separately. However, there are some commonalities between the tests. In each test, I use a directed-mission-member-state-year unit of analysis for all post–Cold War United Nations peacekeeping missions from 1992 to 2015. This means that each UN member state that is not the mission's target country is paired with each mission authorized by the Security Council. Kathman (2013) provides data on member state participation in each mission.[1] To test Hypothesis 1 on the likelihood of *Participation*, I use a probit regression to analyze whether each state participated in a given mission, coded 1 if yes and 0 if no.[2] To test Hypothesis 2 on a state's *Contribution Size*, I use zero-inflated negative binomial (ZINB) models to examine the maximum number of troops a state contributes to each UN peacekeeping mission each year.[3] Contribution sizes range from 0 to over 7,000 (Pakistan in UNOSOM). To test Hypothesis 3, I use a piecewise exponential regression to examine each member's *Duration until Contribution* in months. States that participate at the beginning of the mission are assigned a value of 1. For example, Niger contributed to MINUSMA at its beginning date and thus has a duration of 1. A noncontributing state remains in the data set until it either contributes or the mission ends. Finally, to test Hypothesis 4, I use a piecewise exponential regression to examine a contributing member's *Duration of Contribution* in months, which begins counting the month the state contributes its first solider until the state withdraws its final peacekeeper.

Each of the four analyses uses the same key independent variable, *Ln(Refugee Inflows)*. This variable captures the size of the refugee flows between the country receiving the peacekeeping mission and each potential contributor state in each year of an ongoing mission. By measuring dyadic refugee flows from each conflict area to each potential donor state, I am able to calculate the direct externalities received by each third party from the conflict rather than capturing a general measure of conflict severity, or the overall magnitude of the humanitarian crisis for the international community. I collect data on directed refugee flows for each dyad from the Office of the United Nations High Commissioner for Refugees (UNHCR 2018). I use the natural log of the refugee flows because these dyadic flows are highly skewed. In these data, refugee inflows range from 0 for many dyads—for example, Haiti to Guyana in 2000—to 1.9 million from Afghanistan to Pakistan in 2010. This variable, and all other time-varying independent variables, is lagged one year in the nonduration models.

I compare the effects of these direct refugee inflows to *Ln(Total Refugee Outflows)* to capture the total refugee outflows from each conflict each year (UNHCR 2018). Conflicts that create severe externalities for the international community may be a significant threat to international security. Given this concern, and the humanitarian motives such crises provide potential contributors, crises that produce large numbers of forced migrants may be more likely to see intervention (e.g., Bove and Elia 2011). Higher numbers of total outflows may also mean that those states receiving the refugees may experience high numbers of inflows.

I then compare the effects of these two refugee variables to additional independent variables that capture alternative explanations of these patterns and potential confounding effects that are common across the tests.

First, I consider factors specific to member states. I include whether each member state is a *Democracy* based on the Polity IV scale, from –10 (highly autocratic) to 10 (highly democratic) (Marshall, Gurr, and Jaggers 2017). Extant explanations of peacekeeping expect that democracies will contribute more than other regimes to externalize their domestic norms of peace or to please humanitarian factions within their state (e.g., Lebovic 2004). Therefore, we should expect democracies to participate more often and more quickly, contribute more troops, and remain committed to the mission in an effort to realize the norms they view as important. Also, democracies tend to cluster in "good neighborhoods" that see few civil wars and thus few refugee flows between countries, which may confound the relationship between refugee flows and my behaviors of interest.

I include each member state's logged gross domestic product per capita, *Ln(GDPpc)*, from the Maddison Project Database, version 2018 (Bolt et al. 2018) to capture financial need. States may participate in peacekeeping to help fund their militaries (e.g., Berman and Sams 2000; Victor 2010). If this argument is correct, poorer states should contribute large numbers of troops often and quickly, and keep those troops deployed throughout the missions, to maximize the per solider per month reimbursement provided by the United Nations to participating countries. Furthermore, poor states tend to cluster in bad neighborhoods that often see civil war and high levels of refugee flows, which could confound the relationship between inflows and my measures of participation.

I include each member state's *Ln(Population)* from the Maddison Project Database (Bolt et al. 2018), because more populous states have more people to potentially contribute to peacekeeping missions, given that peacekeeping can work as a jobs program. Larger populations can also strain food and health supplies. Introducing refugee flows can create greater turmoil as these pressures mount.

I include whether a member state is a permanent five (*P5*) member of the UN Security Council, coded 1 if yes and 0 otherwise. The Security Council must authorize UN peacekeeping missions. Including this variable controls for the possibility that the permanent five members may only allow peacekeeping missions in those areas where they have a strategic interest in ending the conflict (Diehl 2008), as the United States did in Haiti. The P5 states tend to be located in better geographical neighborhoods where civil wars and refugee flows are unlikely. However, several of the permanent five Security Council members are also former colonial powers and thus may attract refugee inflows.

Second, I consider factors that are specific to the given mission and target country. I include whether each third-party member state is *Contiguous* to the war-torn country, as coded by Bennett and Stam (2000), to control for the possibility that states are more likely to send troops to nearby conflicts because of a fear of conflict contagion or other geopolitical concerns, regardless of their refugee inflows. Contiguity may also be a confounder because refugees tend to flee to nearby countries.

I include whether a member state possesses a *Joint Ethnicity* with the target state because states may intervene in a conflict to support a regime with which it shares a common ethnicity. Additionally, controlling for joint ethnicity helps ensure that the refugee flow variable is not capturing situations of states aiding those with a common heritage. This variable is coded 1 to all dyads in which the majority of the population in the third-party and war-torn states share a common ethnicity; it is coded 0 for all others (Central Intelligence Agency 2018).

I include a variable for whether each potential contributor and the target state share an *Alliance*, coded 1 if the dyad is an ally and 0 otherwise (Gibler 2009). Allies share common strategic and security interests (Russett and Oneal 2001), and they may be more willing to engage in peacekeeping in a partner state to provide support for the unstable regime (Beardsley and Schmidt 2012).

I include a variable for whether the member state and target state have *Colonial Ties* (Tir et al. 1998) because colonial powers may be more likely to intervene in countries with which they have a history of colonial involvement (Kathman 2011). If not fleeing to a nearby country, refugees are also more likely to seek shelter in a former colonial power (Moore and Shellman 2007). This variable is coded 1 for each dyad in which the target state was a former colony of the potential contributor and 0 for all others.

I include *(Other Contributors)*, which is the count of other states contributing to a mission in each year.[4] Contributions by other states may reduce the number of refugees fleeing the conflict into a state's territory. If the refugee situation can be handled without its involvement, a state is unlikely to waste its soldiers on the conflict.[5]

There are a few important differences between the tests of the four hypotheses in addition to those differences in dependent variable and estimator described above. First, to test Hypothesis 1, I include time polynomials of the number of years, years squared, and years cubed since a state last contributed to a peacekeeping mission to control for temporal dependency in the data.

Second, to test Hypothesis 2, I include each member's lagged contribution size. Not only does including this variable help with problems of autocorrelation in the data, but it also controls for the possibility that some states may participate more in peacekeeping because they already built up the infrastructure to do so in past missions. Additionally, it controls for the possibility that some states may be overstretched militarily and thus be unable to participate in any additional mission.

To test Hypotheses 3 and 4, the piecewise exponential survival models allow the baseline hazard to vary within different time intervals and place few restrictions on duration dependence in the data. It is important to let the baseline hazard rate vary so as not to make potentially untenable assumptions about the data-generating process and thus how actors behave across time. For Hypothesis 3, I divide the time intervals into three piecewise indicator variables to capture the number of months until a country joined the mission—as 1–50 months, 51–100 months, and 101–199 months—where the last period is the reference category. For Hypothesis 4, I divide the time intervals into three piecewise indicator variables to capture the number of months since a country joined the mission—as 1–25 months, 26–75 months, and 76–147 months—where the last period is the reference category. The time intervals for each test are selected by viewing patterns in the data and using goodness-of-fit measures. The models are also robust to choosing other intervals.

Analysis of Hypothesis 1

The first dilemma the United Nations faces in forming a peacekeeping mission is how to attract member states to contribute military personnel to the mission. I argue that states receiving refugee inflows from the mission's target state are more likely to contribute personnel than those states not receiving such inflows. I test this proposition—Hypothesis 1—in Models 1 through 4, which are found in table 3.1. Across these four models, strong support for my argument exists. In Model 1, I compare the effects of each member state's dyadic refugee inflows from the conflict country to

Table 3.1. Probit Analysis of Participation in Each UN Peacekeeping Mission[a]

	Model 1: Base	Model 2: Member Factors	Model 3: Mission Factors	Model 4: Full
	Coefficient (Standard Error)[b]	Coefficient (Standard Error)	Coefficient (Standard Error)	Coefficient (Standard Error)
Ln(Refugee Inflows)$_{t-1}$	0.043* (0.009)	0.042* (0.009)	0.025* (0.011)	0.023* (0.012)
Ln(Total Refugee Outflows)$_{t-1}$	0.033* (0.006)	0.034* (0.007)	0.015 (0.010)	0.015 (0.010)
Democracy$_{t-1}$		0.000 (0.005)		−0.001 (0.006)
Ln(GDPpc)$_{t-1}$		−0.114* (0.023)		−0.088* (0.025)
Ln(Population)$_{t-1}$		0.117* (0.020)		0.146* (0.022)
P5$_{t-1}$		0.018 (0.119)		−0.037 (0.126)
Contiguous			−0.267 (0.192)	−0.417* (0.206)
Joint Ethnicity			−0.500* (0.230)	−0.456 (0.259)
Alliance$_{t-1}$			0.715* (0.106)	0.656* (0.115)
Colonial Ties			0.924* (0.223)	0.974* (0.230)
Ln(Other Contributors)$_{t-1}$			0.464* (0.018)	0.490* (0.019)
Years until Contribution	−0.361* (0.019)	−0.318* (0.022)	−0.353* (0.024)	−0.305* (0.027)
Years until Contribution^2	0.020* (0.003)	0.016* (0.003)	0.019* (0.003)	0.017* (0.004)
Years until Contribution^3	−0.000* (0.000)	−0.000* (0.000)	−0.000* (0.000)	−0.000* (0.000)
Constant	−1.353* (0.071)	−1.492* (0.298)	−2.272* (0.111)	−2.976* (0.341)
N	41,577	32,079	36,707	28,380
Log pseudolikelihood	−8,208.927	−7,638.832	−5,505.002	−5,077.220

[a] $p < 0.05$*.
[b] Errors are clustered by the potential contributor-mission dyad.

those of the conflict's total refugee outflows. This allows me to distinguish the effects of direct inflows to those of the humanitarian crisis as a whole. I find that both direct and total refugee flows increase the probability that member states will contribute. Setting all variables at their means and then increasing *Ln(Refugee Inflows)* from its minimum to its maximum, I find that inflows increase a state's likelihood of participation by 5 percent.[6] I also find that the total outflows from the conflict increase the likelihood that any member state is likely to contribute troops by 2 percent. This pattern supports the expectations of previous scholars that peacekeeping provision is tied to the severity of the humanitarian crisis (Bove and Elia 2011). It also suggests that the shift in the UN's focus to protecting civilian populations is limited not only to the institutional apparatus but also to many of the member states. However, direct inflows are 2.5 times more powerful in attracting contributions than is the magnitude of the humanitarian crisis caused by the conflict. Therefore, the direct externalities experienced by a member state are more important in its calculation of whether to join the mission than is the total humanitarian crisis caused by the conflict.

Two further patterns are worth discussing. The results of Model 1 are additive. A state experiencing direct inflows is also influenced by the total humanitarian crisis of the conflict. However, these results do not consider how these flows influence each other. For further analysis, I consider the interaction between direct and indirect flows.[7] First, I examine how the conflict's total outflows influence a state's participation when it is receiving direct inflows from the war zone. I find that the effect of direct inflows decreases in the presence of global outflows (see panel A of figure 3.1). This suggests that when global flows are low, and others are unlikely to join the mission, the importance of direct flows is heightened for host states, as they understand that they must shoulder the peacekeeping burden to limit further flows into their borders. Second, I examine how direct inflows modify how a member reacts to the conflict's total outflows. Here, a larger number of direct inflows decreases the effect of total refugee flows (see panel B of figure 3.1). *Ln(Total Refugee Outflows)* only increases member contributions when the third party is receiving few direct inflows. This pattern provides three implications. First, humanitarian crises can influence members to contribute troops when they feel little direct cost from the conflict. For instance, despite receiving very few refugees from Somalia, Germany has contributed significantly to the United Nations operation in Somalia (UNOSOM). Second, the magnitude of the humanitarian crisis is not needed

Figure 3.1. Interactive Effects of Direct and Global Refugee Flows

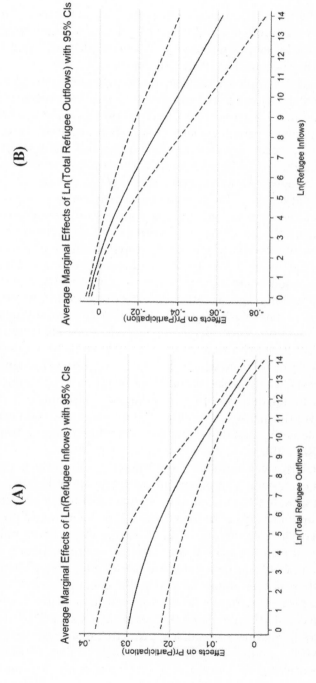

NOTE: Effect denoted by solid line; confidence intervals denoted by dashed lines.

to motivate member participation when they are directly experiencing costs from the conflict. Third, however, if host states understand the magnitude of the humanitarian crises and believe others will contribute to the mission, they become less likely to contribute.

In Model 2, I compare the effects of refugee inflows and total refugee flows to other features of the member state that are expected to influence participation. Here I find that direct inflows increase the likelihood of participation by 7 percent, whereas total refugee outflows increase participation by 3 percent. A state's population size also increases its likelihood of contributing troops by 9 percent. Further analysis reveals that the effect of direct refugee inflows is statistically significant and increasing along with population size. This suggests that when a state is receiving inflows and has a larger population, it may face more strain on its food and health supplies from the combination of citizens and migrants it now supports, thus increasing its willingness to help stop the refugee-producing conflict. However, states with the largest populations (e.g., China and India) tend to have other resources to handle the inflows. Conversely, the effect of population size is only significant when direct refugee inflows are low. This suggests that states with large populations use peacekeeping as a way to export labor. Thus, these effects help us understand contribution patterns by states like Bangladesh and Pakistan, which send large numbers of troops abroad to countries from which they are not experiencing significant refugee inflows (Gleason-Roberts 2012). For instance, as of March 2018, Pakistan and Bangladesh were the two largest contributors to the United Nations Multidimensional Integrated Stabilization Mission in the Central African Republic, despite neither receiving direct inflows from this conflict (DPKO 2018a).

Conversely, wealthier states are 7 percent less likely to contribute to these same missions. This pattern fits with previous scholarship that views the UN's subsidy to contributors as its main method of attracting participation from poor states like Bangladesh (e.g., Bobrow and Boyer 1997). It is important to note that the effect of refugee inflows is significant across the range of state wealth but decreases as wealth increases. This makes sense given that wealthier states are often better able to handle refugee inflows than poorer states. Similarly, the effect of wealth is significant across the range of refugee inflows. However, an increase in refugee inflows further decreases the likelihood that a wealthier state will participate in the peacekeeping mission. Instead, it appears that wealthier states prefer to go it alone when a conflict directly threatens their borders. A common refrain in the peacekeeping literature is that poor states are more likely to

Figure 3.2. Interactive Effects of Wealth and Direct Refugee Flows

(A)   (B)

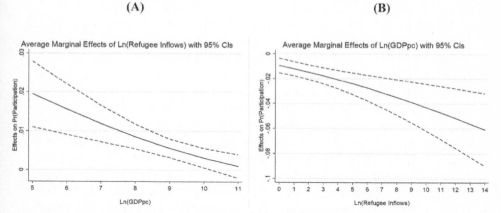

NOTE: Effect denoted by solid line; confidence intervals denoted by dashed lines.

contribute than wealthy states because they rent out their soldiers to do most of the UN's peacekeeping work (Berman and Sams 2000; Bobrow and Boyer 1997; Bove and Elia 2011; Victor 2010). However, these interactive results, which are presented in figure 3.2, suggest that many of these poor contributors are driven by their need to stop further refugee flows across their borders.

Two results of this model are important to note, given their statistical insignificance. First, I find that democracies are no more likely to participate in any given UN peacekeeping mission than are nondemocracies (Lebovic 2004). Daniel (2011) suggests that the UN should draw more heavily from democracies interested in promoting a Western agenda globally when trying to fulfill its mandated troop levels, and Bellamy and Williams (2013) note that it is important for these Western democracies to contribute, as they have better military capabilities to assist the UN. However, my results indicate that democratic interests are similar to those of nondemocracies: they are not likely to become involved in peacekeeping unless the crisis threatens them directly. And the effect of refugee inflows is statistically significant and relatively stable across the range of regime types. Second, the permanent five members of the UN Security Council are no more or less likely to contribute to their peacekeeping missions than are other member states. Thus, though the P5 is crucial to authorizing these missions, they are not providing the manpower. Instead, they tend to provide the financial support for the mission. The P5 rank among the top six financial contributors to the UN budget (DPKO 2014), but China's presence in Darfur and the United States in Haiti and Somalia are not common occurrences.

In Model 3, I compare direct refugee inflows and the conflict's total outflows with other influences of the target country. In this model, I continue to find that direct inflows increase the likelihood of participation— here, by 12 percent. However, the conflict's total flows are no longer statistically significant, suggesting that, as I expected, the direct ramifications of the conflict for a state are more important for its behavior than the crisis as a whole. Similarly, a state's geographical proximity is not statistically significant. This result holds when refugee inflows are dropped from the model, indicating that these variables are not proxies for each other. Note that the effect of inflows is significant for noncontiguous states, while the effect of contiguity is never significant along the size of the inflows. The other mission-specific factors are each statistically significant predictors of participation. Of these, only joint ethnicity reduces the likelihood of participation—by less than 1 percent. Importantly, the effect of refugee inflows is only significant when the states do not share a joint ethnicity. Furthermore, the negative relationship between joint ethnicity and contribution is significant across the range of inflow size. These patterns suggest that some of *Ln(Refugee Inflows)*'s influence operates through the threat of shifting or exacerbating conflictual demographics within the state due to nonethnic kin arriving within the country's borders.

Alliances, former colonizers, and the presence of other contributors increase the likelihood that a third party contributes troops to a given mission by 3, 6, and 8 percent, respectively. These results indicate that military considerations influence how states react to conflicts (e.g., Mueller 2004), even when they engage in peacekeeping instead of unilateral military intervention. I have argued that states use peacekeeping rather than unilateral intervention to gain legitimacy for their actions when attempting to prevent further refugee inflows across their borders. My logic fits well with these patterns emphasizing the military and strategic calculations made by members when contributing troops. Figure 3.3 plots the mean first difference effects for direct refugee inflows compared with each of these other conflict-specific factors after moving each variable from its minimum to its maximum value, holding all others at their means. As is evident from figure 3.3, preventing refugee inflows plays a significant role in a state's calculation relative to other conflict-specific factors.

Furthermore, additional analysis reveals that the effect of refugee inflows is only important when an alliance is not present and that the effect

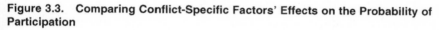

Figure 3.3. Comparing Conflict-Specific Factors' Effects on the Probability of Participation

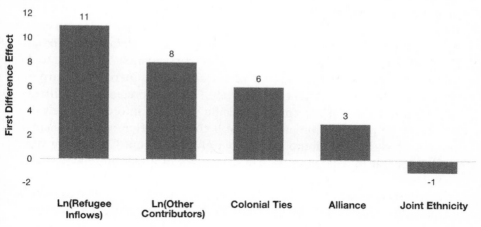

of the alliance is only significant when the member is receiving few refugee inflows. Therefore, these are substitutive mechanisms rather than complementary ones. For example, Russia contributed to the United Nations Mission in Tajikistan despite receiving no refugees from the conflict. The colonial mechanism works in a similar manner, in that the effect of refugee inflows is only important when the member was not a former colonizer of the target country and that the effect of the colonial relationship is only significant when the member is receiving few refugee inflows. For example, France participated in the United Nations Mission in the Central African Republic despite receiving fewer than seventy refugees from the conflict each year. The "other contributors" mechanism works in the opposite manner. The contributions of other states do not deter a state from contributing to peacekeeping. Instead of free-riding on other members, a state becomes more willing to share the burden of peacekeeping as others contribute to a mission. Furthermore, the effect of direct refugee inflows is most pronounced when several states are contributing. The other states' efforts help reassure the host state that there is enough support for the operation to make the mission a success. The effect of the other contributors is increasing along with a state's refugee inflows.

Model 4 simultaneously compares direct and total refugee flows to both member-specific and conflict-specific factors. Here, direct refugee inflows continue to have a statistically significant influence on increasing the likelihood that a member state participates. However, total refugee flows do not. When combining member- and conflict-specific factors into one model, I find that both sets of elements influence whether a given member state contributes troops to the UN mission. However, this decision appears to be dominated by the conflict-specific issues. Other contributors, colonial ties, and alliances increase the likelihood of participation by 13, 9, and 4 percent, respectively, while population size and wealth increase this probability by only 6 and 2 percent, respectively. Furthermore, including direct refugee inflows and other conflict-specific variables into our models of peacekeeping participation provides for better prediction of which members are likely to contribute troops to a given mission. Comparing the receiver operating characteristic (ROC) curves of a baseline model that includes only total refugee outflows and the member-specific factors to a fully specified model, I find that the model including the conflict-specific factors outperforms the baseline significantly. The area under the curve for the baseline model is 0.8147, whereas the curve for the fully specified Model 4 is 0.9071, as shown in figure 3.4. This difference is statistically significant at the 99 percent level.

Figure 3.4. ROC Curves Comparing Model 4 to a Member-Specific Baseline

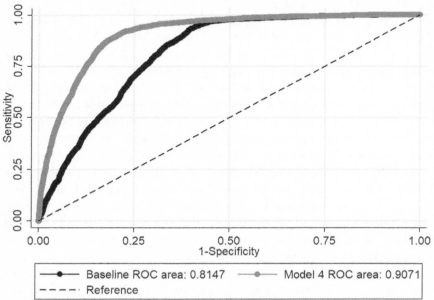

Analysis of Hypothesis 2

In addition to increasing the likelihood of participation, I posit that direct refugee inflows from the conflict country influence the size of a third-party member country's troop contribution to the mission. Specifically, Hypothesis 2 states, "A state is likely to contribute more troops to peacekeeping missions in situations from which it is experiencing higher volumes of refugee inflows." To test this hypothesis, I utilize a zero-inflated negative binomial (ZINB) model. Because a significant number of states never participate in UN peacekeeping operations, it is likely that two populations exist—a peacekeeping set of members (e.g., Bangladesh and Canada) and a nonpeacekeeping set of members (e.g., Bhutan and Cuba). Therefore, the ZINB presents tests of two stages. The first is a "certain zero" population that never contributes to peacekeeping. States in this population will always have a contribution size of zero. The first stage of this model estimates how likely a state is to never participate in a given peacekeeping mission by using a logistic regression of the variables I found to be statistically significant predictors of participation in Models 1 through 4. The second stage is of a population that sometimes participates. States in this population will have contribution sizes that vary depending on the incentives the state faces for each mission. Taking into account the predictions of this first stage and the actors that never participate in peacekeeping, the second stage uses a negative binominal model to estimate how many troops a given state is likely to contribute to a particular mission, estimated across the full range of independent variables.

Table 3.2 presents Models 5 through 8, which test Hypothesis 2 using the ZINB. Across these four models, I do not find support for Hypothesis 2. In Models 5, 6, and 8, I find *Ln(Refugee Inflows)* to be statistically insignificant. In Model 7, direct refugee inflows are significant but suggest that a unit change in the logged count of incoming refugees decreases the size of a state's contribution to the given mission by 7 percent.[8] Although quantitative support is lacking for Hypothesis 2, qualitative support exists. For example, after receiving nearly 2,000 refugees from the conflict in Sierra Leone, Nigeria contributed over 3,000 soldiers to the United Nations Mission in Sierra Leone. Similarly, near the end of the mission in Sierra Leone, Nigeria received over 6,000 refugees from the Liberian conflict and also contributed nearly 2,000 troops to the United Nations Mission in Liberia.

Table 3.2. Zero-Inflated Negative Binominal of Contributions to Each UN Peacekeeping Mission[a]

	Model 5: Base		Model 6: Member Factors		Model 7: Mission Factors		Model 8: Full	
	Stage 1: Never Participate	Stage 2: Size of Contribution	Stage 1: Never Participate	Stage 2: Size of Contribution	Stage 1: Never Participate	Stage 2: Size of Contribution	Stage 1: Never Participate	Stage 2: Size of Contribution
	Coefficient (Standard Error)[b]	Coefficient (Standard Error)	Coefficient (Standard Error)	Coefficient (Standard Error)	Coefficient (Standard Error)	Coefficient (Standard Error)	Coefficient (Standard Error)	Coefficient (Standard Error)
Ln(Refugee Inflows)$_{t-1}$	-0.280* (0.041)	0.024 (0.037)	-0.214* (0.043)	-0.006 (0.029)	-0.075* (0.023)	-0.075* (0.033)	-0.059* (0.030)	-0.027 (0.041)
Ln(Total Refugee Outflows)$_{t-1}$	-0.181* (0.034)	0.060 (0.047)	-0.182* (0.033)	-0.023 (0.040)	0.937 (0.555)	0.223* (0.033)		0.357* (0.062)
Democracy$_{t-1}$				-0.032* (0.015)				-0.002 (0.019)
Ln(GDPpc)$_{t-1}$			0.205* (0.103)	-0.200 (0.081)			0.195* (0.091)	-0.214 (0.131)
Ln(Population)$_{t-1}$			-0.374* (0.073)	0.234* (0.062)			-0.311* (0.058)	0.249* (0.095)
P5$_{t-1}$				0.142 (0.425)				-0.479 (0.399)
Contiguous						0.804* (0.390)	0.661 (0.571)	0.265 (0.531)
Joint Ethnicity						-1.800* (0.411)	-1.227* (0.236)	-1.440* (0.444)
Alliance$_{t-1}$					-1.451* (0.234)	0.897* (0.189)		0.281 (0.250)

Colonial Ties					-1.547* (0.618)	0.851 (0.443)	-1.637* (0.557)	0.297 (0.623)
Ln(Other Contributors)$_{t-1}$	1.694* (0.155)				-1.360* (0.072)	-0.943* (0.118)	-1.588* (0.071)	-1.674* (0.165)
Years until Contribution	-0.126* (0.019)		1.273* (0.155)		0.998* (0.090)		0.928* (0.092)	
Years until Contribution²	0.003* (0.001)		-0.087* (0.018)		-0.058* (0.012)		-0.057* (0.012)	
Years until Contribution³			0.002* (0.001)		0.001* (0.000)		0.001* (0.000)	
Ln(Previous Contribution)		0.732* (0.029)		0.005* (0.000)		0.004* (0.000)		0.792* (0.047)
Constant	0.296 (0.424)	1.098* (0.543)	2.857* (1.301)	2.360* (1.191)	3.599* (0.169)	3.276* (0.452)	5.357* (1.109)	2.047 (1.770)
α	23.086* (1.496)		20.455* (1.851)			9.840* (0.956)		7.161* (0.592)
N	41,577		32,079		34,417		28,380	
Log pseudolikelihood	-23,588.83		-22,767.83		-18,080.95		-16,789.24	

[a] p < 0.05.

[b] Errors are clustered by the potential contributor-mission dyad.

Why is there this disconnect between the quantitative results and the case studies? One reason is that sometimes an interested member's ability to contribute significant numbers of troops to a mission is blocked by the political interests of the target country. For instance, in 2007, at the start of the United Nations Mission in Darfur, Egypt received over 10,000 refugees from Sudan. In response, Egypt desired to send three infantry battalions to Sudan. However, the Darfuri rebels, understanding the political and strategic interests Egypt possessed for participating in the mission, pressured the UN to limit Egypt's involvement in the conflict management (Henke 2016). Therefore, the direct link between refugee inflows and contribution size may be obscured by behind-the-scenes bargaining between the UN and the belligerents.

The other variables in this analysis present similarly mixed patterns. Model 6 indicates that democratic and wealthier states tend to contribute fewer troops by 3 and 18 percent respectively, while more populous states contribute 26 percent more troops than other states. However, Model 8, after accounting for the other alternative explanations and confounders, indicates that population size is the only significant member-specific factor. When coupled with the analysis of Hypothesis 1, these results indicate that peacekeeping contribution works similarly to a jobs program for populous states because they are more likely to get involved and send larger numbers of personnel to war zones around the globe.

In these models, conflict- and mission-specific factors do not fare much better. Model 7 indicates that while contiguous states and allies tend to contribute 103 and 145 percent more troops than others, respectively, further highlighting the importance of military considerations in the decision to engage in peacekeeping, members sharing an ethnicity with the target state contribute roughly 80 percent fewer troops and 60 percent fewer personnel for a unit increase in (logged) other contributors. However, after accounting for the other alternative explanations and confounders, Model 8 reveals that only joint ethnicity and the size of others' contributions continue to influence a member's participation. Taking into account the previous analysis, it appears that the pattern in decreasing contributions relative to those of others is likely due to burden sharing between the increasing number of contributors rather than free-riding on each other.

Across these models, *Ln(Total Refugee Outflows)* also displays inconsistent behavior. Only in Models 7 and 8 does the severity of the humanitarian crisis appear to increase the size of members' contributions. Note that these models are the ones that account for conflict-specific factors. It appears that we can only account for the influence of humanitarian crises once we have netted out those strategic and military concerns that also influence a member's participation. Further analysis also reveals that, as with the question of whether a state participates, the scale of the humanitarian crisis increases a member's contribution size only when it is not receiving significant direct refugee inflows from the conflict. Once again, then, direct and total refugee inflows appear to be substitute mechanisms for influencing a member's participation with an ongoing mission.

Across all the models, a state's previous contributions to a given mission influence its subsequent contributions. Those states that send large contingents of troops in one year of the mission often send larger contingents of troops in subsequent years. This reinforces the idea that states focus their contributions on specific missions. Furthermore, when also analyzing a state's previous total contributions to all ongoing UN peacekeeping missions, I find no evidence suggesting that some states are simply large contributors across the UN's missions. Instead, patterns in the size of contribution tend to be dictated by factors related to a given mission rather than overall peacekeeping efforts. However, overall, these models provide little insight into the determinants of a member's contribution size. It appears that we have a much better understanding of who participates rather than the extent to which they contribute. This is clearly an important avenue of research for future scholars to more fully explore, as the United Nations struggles to reach its mandated troop levels.

Analysis of Hypothesis 3

The second dilemma the United Nations faces in forming a peacekeeping mission is how to motivate member states to contribute quickly to a mission. I argue that states receiving refugee inflows from the mission's target state are likely to contribute personnel more quickly to the mission than those states not receiving such inflows. I test this proposition—Hypothesis 3—in Models 9 through 12, which are found in table 3.3. Across these four models, strong support for my argument exists.

In Model 9, I compare the effects of each member state's dyadic refugee inflows from the conflict country with those of the conflict's total refugee outflows. As with the previous analyses, this allows me to distinguish the effects of direct inflows from those of the humanitarian crisis as a whole. Here Model 9 predicts that a 1-unit increase in the logged count of refugee inflows increases the likelihood that a state will contribute to a specific

Table 3.3. Survival Analysis of the Time until Participation in UN Peacekeeping Missions[a]

	Model 9: Base	Model 10: Member Specific	Model 11: Mission Specific	Model 12: Full
	Coefficient (Standard Error)[b]	Coefficient (Standard Error)	Coefficient (Standard Error)	Coefficient (Standard Error)
Ln(Refugee Inflows)	0.176*	0.103*	0.239*	0.100*
	(0.010)	(0.013)	(0.017)	(0.021)
Ln(Total Refugee Outflows)	0.007	0.021	−0.069*	−0.034
	(0.011)	(0.012)	(0.017)	(0.019)
Democracy		0.057*		0.060*
		(0.007)		(0.008)
Ln(GDPpc)		−0.077*		−0.058
		(0.033)		(0.041)
Ln(Population)		0.353*		0.402*
		(0.024)		(0.032)
P5		0.085		0.124
		(0.154)		(0.195)
Contiguous			−1.673*	−0.830*
			(0.296)	(0.342)
Joint Ethnicity			−0.695*	−0.747
			(0.343)	(0.384)
Alliance			0.467*	0.864*
			(0.176)	(0.190)
Colonial Ties			2.392*	2.256*
			(0.339)	(0.340)
Ln(Other Contributors)			1.110*	1.153*
			(0.048)	(0.051)
0–50 Months	3.384*	3.361*	3.063*	2.973*
	(0.320)	(0.322)	(0.579)	(0.581)
51–100 Months	0.599	0.607	0.314	0.256
	(0.374)	(0.377)	(0.616)	(0.619)
Constant	−9.541*	−12.305*	−11.369*	−15.004*
	(0.344)	(0.483)	(0.624)	(0.767)
N	48,265	36,467	42,080	31,977
Log pseudolikelihood	−4,806.686	−4,296.460	−3,526.481	−3,098.696

[a] $p < 0.05$*.
[b] Errors are clustered by potential contributor-mission dyad.

mission roughly 20 percent sooner in the given period than other states.[9] Therefore, states hosting refugees from the conflict zone are more likely to contribute and contribute more quickly than other states. Canada, for example, hosted nearly 500 refugees from Haiti in 2004 and immediately participated in the United Nations Stabilization Mission in Haiti once the mission began. However, the scale of the global refugee crisis caused by the target conflict does not influence the speed at which contribution occurs. These results highlight the relative importance of direct flows compared with global flows for each member state.

Panel A of figure 3.5 depicts these patterns well by plotting the survival functions of Model 9 after considering a standard deviation increase in both *Ln(Refugee Inflows)* and *Ln(Total Refugee Outflows)*. These survival functions depict the conditional survival rate describing the risk of a member contributing to a UN operation, given that the mission has lasted to a given point. These postestimation graphs allow us to compare states experiencing a standard deviation increase in each variable of interest. A comparison of the curves in panel A of figure 3.5 clearly indicates that states receiving an increased number of refugee inflows are likely to contribute sooner to a given mission than are other states because the survival rate for these states sits well below that of other states, whereas conflicts producing an increased number of total refugee outflows cause members to hesitate in joining an ongoing mission.

However, as in Model 1, further analysis reveals that the effect of direct inflows is decreasing as the total humanitarian crisis increases, suggesting that in worse crises, members receiving inflows hesitate to respond to the conflict before others join the mission. This pattern can best be depicted by examining the survival functions of the interaction between a standard deviation in *Ln(Refugee Inflows)* and *Ln(Total Refugee Outflows)*. Panel B of figure 3.5 presents this interaction. As is evident from this figure's panel B, the situation in which the conflict only presents an increase in direct refugee inflows for a member sees the member contribute most quickly to the mission, whereas the situation in which the conflict produces both direct inflows for a member and larger numbers of global refugees sees the members hesitate the most in contributing to the mission.

Model 10 compares the refugee variables with the member-specific factors. Model 10 predicts that host states will contribute 11 percent more quickly to a mission than others and that global flows will not influence the speed at which a state contributes. However, some member-specific factors do influence the timing of contributions. In line with my analysis of Hypothesis 1, I find that states with larger populations both are more

Figure 3.5. Survival Functions after a Standard Deviation Increase in Direct and Global Refugee Flows

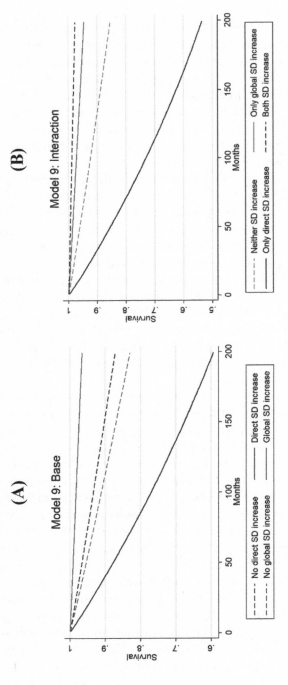

likely to contribute and are likely to participate sooner than other states. Similarly, supporting the initial analysis, I find that wealthier states are not only less likely to participate but are also slower to get involved in any given mission. Additional analysis reveals that wealthier states are also slower to respond to direct refugee inflows than less well-endowed states. This pattern provides further evidence that wealthier states have less need to work through the UN to handle such forced migration on their borders.

Unlike the initial analysis, however, I find that though democracies are no more likely to contribute than nondemocracies, they do tend to contribute quickly if they are going to become involved in a mission. This pattern provides a nuanced understanding of democratic contributions and provides conclusions at odds with previous arguments that democracies participate broadly in peacekeeping missions. Instead, this pattern better fits a logic of democratic military strategy from the interstate war literature, which posits that when democracies decide to send troops abroad, they must act quickly to end the conflict before domestic war weariness occurs (e.g., Reiter and Stam 1998). Furthermore, it appears that non-P5 members respond most quickly to the threats caused by refugee inflows. For example, despite receiving nearly 2,500 refugees from Haiti at the time the United Nations Mission in Haiti was formed, France waited a year and a half to contribute to the mission.

Model 11 introduces the mission-specific variables. Once controlling for these potential confounders, I find that both direct refugee inflows and global flows from the conflict influence the timing of a member's contribution. However, these effects are in opposition. Although direct flows decrease the duration a state waits before contributing by nearly 30 percent, total flows from the conflict increase the duration a member waits before participating by 7 percent. Fortna (2008) has shown that crises producing larger refugee outflows are more likely to receive peacekeeping. Bove and Elia (2011) similarly find that as humanitarian crises start to present a larger threat to international peace and security in terms of forced migration, third parties are more likely to contribute peacekeepers to help handle the situation. Contrary to these expectations, I find that the total level of forced migration decreases the speed at which third parties become willing to participate in a peacekeeping mission. Such a logic squares with Gent's (2007) claim that global humanitarian crises create incentives for free-riding, whereas a direct threat motivates participation. This result suggests that it is the pains directly felt by states receiving the refugee inflows, rather than the overall crisis, that motivate and determine the timing of these states' contributions to peacekeeping efforts. This finding fits with the logic of collective action: although ending the humanitarian crisis may be a public good for the international community in terms of peace and security, states that are not directly affected by the crisis prefer to let others shoulder the costs of peacekeeping.

Similarly, the mission-specific variables influence a state's decision in different directions. Although the risk that a contiguous state or one sharing an ethnicity with the target state contributes to decreases by 81 and 50 percent, respectively, compared with their peers, allies (59 percent) and former colonial powers (about 900 percent) are each likely to contribute more quickly than other states. It also appears that contribution is communal. When some member states contribute quickly, others follow suit. Model 11 predicts that a 1-unit increase in the logged number of other contributors increases the likelihood that another member will join the mission sooner by over 200 percent. Thus, it is important for the UN to incentivize quick participation to both rapidly contain the conflict and to ensure further participation by other member states.

Model 12 provides a fully specified analysis of the timing of contributions. It confirms the results of Models 9 through 11—with two exceptions. First, once the other confounders are included in this model, joint ethnicity is no longer statistically significant. This fits with the results of Model 4 that joint ethnicity does not influence participation in a given peacekeeping mission. Second, Model 12 now indicates that wealthier states are no slower to respond to the UN's call for peacekeepers than are poorer states. This suggests that poor states are not rushing into making a contribution in an effort to maximize every dollar they can take from the UN for their troops' efforts abroad, relative to wealthier states.

Overall, the patterns presented in Models 9 through 12 suggest that the direct costs created by the conflict are a significant motivation for third parties to overcome the collective action problem of peacekeeping and contribute quickly to missions. It appears that appealing to colonial history is one of the best ways to attract contributors because this history creates enough incentives so these states do not need the pressures of direct conflict externalities to participate quickly. Figure 3.6 graphs the survival functions from the base model (Model 9, in panel A of the figure) and the fully specified model (Model 12, in panel B of the figure). Considering these figures together allows us to compare states experiencing a standard deviation increase in refugee inflows from the target country with those without such inflows, without and with controlling for other member- and conflict-specific factors. A comparison of the curves in panels A and B of figure 3.6 clearly indicates that states receiving an increased number of

Figure 3.6. Survival Functions from Exponential Models of Peacekeeper Contributions

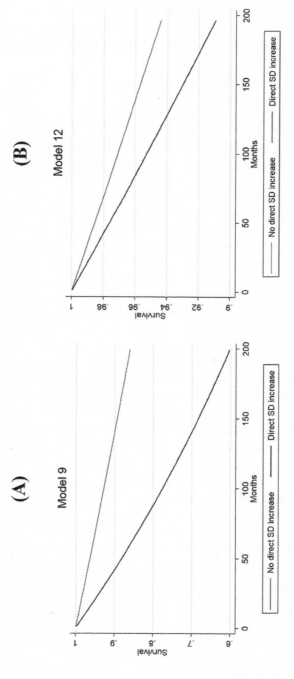

refugee inflows are likely to contribute sooner to a given mission than are other states because the survival rate for these states sits well below that of other states, regardless of the other variables included in these models.

Analysis of Hypothesis 4

The third dilemma the United Nations faces in forming a peacekeeping mission is how to keep member states committed to an ongoing mission. I argue that those states that are continuing to receive refugee inflows from the mission's target state are more likely to withdraw early from the mission than those states not receiving such inflows. I test this proposition—Hypothesis 4—in Models 13 through 16, which are presented in table 3.4. Across these four models, strong support for my argument exists. In Model 13, I compare the effects of each member state's dyadic refugee inflows from the conflict country with those of the conflict's total refugee outflows. As I expect, the model predicts that for each 1-unit increase in logged dyadic inflows, a member is 2 percent more likely to withdraw from the mission. Conversely, the model predicts that for each 1-unit increase in the severity of the humanitarian crisis, a member state is 3 percent less likely to withdraw from the mission. Therefore, dyadic and global refugee flows from a conflict have divergent effects on a member's commitment to the mission. Further analysis reveals that these variables also modify each other. Specifically, the effect of dyadic inflows decreasing the duration of a member's participation is strongest when the global crisis is most severe. This pattern suggests that the member uses the global situation to help gauge the likelihood that its situation will continue to deteriorate. Conversely, the effect of global outflows increasing the duration of a member's participation is strongest when dyadic inflows are low. This suggests that broader humanitarian concerns begin to take a back seat to direct political concerns in the face of greater threat.

In Model 14, I compare the effects of refugee inflows and total refugee flows with other features of the member state that are expected to influence when the state withdraws from an ongoing mission. Here, I find that direct inflows increase the likelihood of withdrawal in a given period by 2 percent, whereas total refugee outflows decrease the likelihood of withdrawal by 3 percent. Model 14 also reveals that wealthier states are 4 percent more likely to withdraw in a given period, while P5 members are 10 percent less likely to leave the mission early. The withdrawal behavior of

Table 3.4. Survival Analysis of the Time until Withdrawal from UN Peacekeeping Missions[a]

	Model 13: Base	Model 14: Member Specific	Model 15: Conflict Specific	Model 16: Full
	Coefficient (Standard Error)[b]	Coefficient (Standard Error)	Coefficient (Standard Error)	Coefficient (Standard Error)
Ln(Refugee Inflows)	0.017* (0.006)	0.019* (0.006)	0.039* (0.010)	0.038* (0.011)
Ln(Total Refugee Outflows)	−0.027* (0.010)	−0.026* (0.011)	−0.035* (0.015)	−0.030* (0.015)
Democracy		−0.005 (0.004)		−0.014* (0.006)
Ln(GDPpc)		0.038* (0.018)		0.068* (0.029)
Ln(Population)		0.016 (0.013)		0.002 (0.024)
P5		−0.140* (0.069)		−0.148 (0.102)
Contiguous			−0.178 (0.223)	−0.122 (0.223)
Joint Ethnicity			0.553* (0.234)	0.707* (0.300)
Alliance			−0.152 (0.104)	−0.196 (0.119)
Colonial Ties			−0.216 (0.154)	−0.185 (0.156)
Ln(Other Contributors)			−0.314* (0.048)	−0.323* (0.047)
0–25 Month Period	2.539* (0.039)	2.547* (0.041)	3.448* (0.134)	3.442* (0.135)
26–75 Month Period	0.937* (0.037)	0.935* (0.039)	1.576* (0.140)	1.563* (0.141)
Constant	−4.499* (0.120)	−4.991* (0.257)	−4.370* (0.240)	−4.928* (0.483)
N	3,396	3,300	2,508	2,446
Log pseudolikelihood	−985.600	−948.365	−682.398	−658.642

[a] $p < 0.05$*.

[b] Errors are clustered by the mission dyad in all models.

wealthier states conforms with the more general patterns in their participation because wealthier states are less likely to participate or get involved
quickly. In general, then, poor states tend to shoulder much of the peacekeeping burden throughout different periods of an operation. Conversely,
the P5 states remain more committed to an ongoing mission than their
wealthy peers or poor states. In all other aspects of peacekeeping participation, the P5 states displayed no observable pattern to distinguish themselves from other states. However, it appears that when a P5 state decides
to contribute to a mission, it makes this commitment for the operation's
long haul.

However, three important member-specific factors modify the relationship between direct inflows and the likelihood of early withdrawal. First,
democracies are more sensitive to the effects of continued inflows. Although
democracy has no independent effect on the likelihood of withdrawal, it
exacerbates a state's willingness to leave the mission due to refugee inflows
before the job is complete. This is likely because democratic leaders feel
more domestic pressure to return troops home and seek alternative solutions to the pressures created by a refugee influx. This result again fits well
with our understanding of democratic military deployment more than
with previous claims about democratic peacekeeping behavior. Similarly,
wealthier states are also more likely to withdraw from the mission when
facing continued refugee inflows. This is likely because wealthier states
have a greater array of options from which they can choose rather than
continuing to send peacekeepers to a mission that is not producing the
results they desire. Therefore, the wealthy democracies that have the capacity to remain committed to the UN's peacekeeping missions over the long
term are the ones that are most likely to leave as the mission struggles. For
example, France withdrew in less than a year and a half from missions in
the Central African Republic and Chad, in Haiti, and in the Côte d'Ivoire
despite receiving over 1,000 refugees from each of these countries in the
year it exited each mission.

In Model 15, I again find the pattern that direct inflows promote early
withdraw (4 percent), while larger global flows keep states committed to
the mission (3 percent). Model 15 also indicates that though members sharing a joint ethnicity with the target states are 74 percent more likely to
withdraw in a given period, members generally are 27 percent less likely
to withdraw as the number of other contributors increases. Thus, across all
models probing different aspects of the peacekeeping participation puzzle,

a general theme has developed that contribution is driven by both indi-vidualistic and communal factors. Though direct conflict externalities greatly shape whether any given member participates and remains com-mitted to an operation, it appears that states adjust their behavior based on the behavior of their peers. Other contributors increase the likelihood that a member will participate, get involved quickly, and remain committed to a given mission. However, larger contributions by others influence a mem-ber to contribute less. Together, these patterns suggest that the communal nature of peacekeeping is not a story about norm adoption but one about burden sharing, as the members of the international community work together to secure peace and security globally.

As with the member-specific factors, several conflict-specific factors modify the relationship between refugee inflows and withdrawal. First, the effects of refugee inflows are strongest in noncontiguous states and those without a previous colonial history vis-à-vis the target, suggesting that without other geopolitical interests at stake, refugee inflows will have a greater influence in driving a state from the mission. A similar effect exists for states that do not share a joint ethnicity with the target country. However, both members allied and not allied to the target states react similarly to the pressures of refugee inflows. Finally, I find that the effects of refugee inflows are strongest when there are more contributors to the mission. This suggests that states receiving direct inflows find it more valuable to work outside the United Nations when other states are shoul-dering the UN burden. In line with this logic, I also find that the effect of other contributors keeping a member committed to the mission only holds when that member is not receiving significant refugee inflows from the target state.

Model 16 compares the two types of refugee flows with both member-specific and mission-specific factors. This model confirms the findings of the disaggregated models: direct flows increase the risk of withdrawal, while total flows decrease the risk of withdrawal. Comparing the hazard ratios produced by Model 16 in figure 3.7, it appears that the statistically significant refugee variables (refugee inflows and total outflows), member-specific variables (democracy and wealth), and conflict-specific variables (other contributors) each exert similarly sized influences on the decision whether to withdraw early from a mission. Only joint ethnicity appears to produce a noticeably higher degree of influence on this decision. However, this effect also displays the widest variance of all the variables.

Figure 3.7. Factors Influencing the Duration of Participation

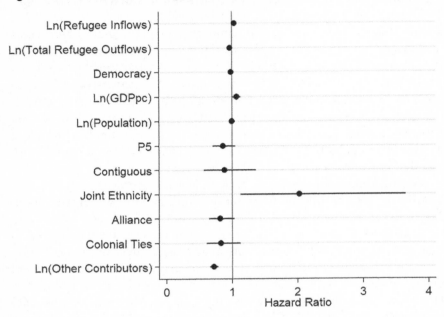

The United Nations Mission in Sudan, 2005–11

To clarify some of the dynamics presented in the empirical results, I consider contribution patterns to the United Nations Mission in Sudan (UNMIS), which lasted from 2005 to 2011. Between 1983 and 2005, Sudan experienced civil war between the predominantly Arabic and Muslim North and the predominantly African and non-Muslim South after the failure of the Addis Ababa Agreement. In 2005—under the auspices of the Intergovernmental Authority on Development, and with strong support from Norway, the United Kingdom, and the United States—the government of Sudan and the Sudan People's Liberation Movement/Army signed the Comprehensive Peace Agreement (CPA). The CPA was complex and was to be implemented over a six-year period (July 2005–July 2011). It called for the establishment of a Government of National Unity and an autonomous Government of South Sudan, with democratic elections, until the South was to hold a referendum on its independence in January 2011. Additionally, a cease-fire was to be immediate, with Northern and

Southern soldiers returning home to a disarmament, demobilization, and reintegration process. The CPA explicitly requested international support, and less than three months after the agreement was signed, the UN Security Council authorized UNMIS. The UNMIS mandate specifically referred to the promotion of human rights, to protecting civilians, and the need to return refugees to the country. Furthermore, the UNMIS mandate was authorized under Chapter VII of the UN Charter, authorizing UN peacekeepers to use force to, inter alia, protect the civilian population. However, despite unanimous support from the Security Council, UNMIS was slow to deploy and member states never contributed enough soldiers to meet the mission's mandated troop levels (Hansen 2015). Thus, the experience of UNMIS helps highlight the UN's dilemmas in attracting participants and getting them to the field quickly.

Who contributed to UNMIS? Over the course of the mission, 52 UN members contributed troops. Several patterns are evident in the list of contributors. A total of 39 contributors (or 75 percent) were receiving refugee inflows from Sudan before the onset of UNMIS, and 47 (90 percent) of the contributors received refugees from Sudan by the beginning of the peacekeeping operation. These patterns are supportive of my theory: states receiving refugees from Sudan contributed to the peacekeeping operation within Sudan. Egypt's participation in UNMIS best exemplifies the logic. Egypt was hosting roughly 15,000 Sudanese refugees by the start of UNMIS. The refugees coming from Sudan had frequently engaged in protests against Egypt, and turmoil was brewing in the country. Repatriating these refugees became a pressing security concern. When UNMIS was announced, Egypt's parliament unanimously approved President Hosni Mubarak's request to contribute troops to the UN mission, emphasizing that stabilizing Sudan was critical for ensuring Egypt's security (Deutsche Presse Agentur 2005). However, it is also important to remember the 10 percent of participants that were not hosting Sudanese refugees. These states, like Bangladesh, help reinforce the empirical results discussed above that multiple processes bring states to contribute to a given mission.

How much did the states contribute to UNMIS? As with the econometric results, the UNMIS case reveals several reasons for the number of troops each state sent. Egypt, for example, ranked in the top five contributors to UNMIS. This fits my argument. However, the other top four contributors participating in UNMIS were not driven by refugee concerns as much as Egypt. Nigeria and Rwanda each received refugees from Sudan, but much less than Egypt. Instead, their contributions were driven by

Sudanese president Omar al-Bashir's demands that the peacekeeping personnel be predominantly from African states (Hansen 2015). Note, however, that these African states were not contiguous with Sudan, supporting the empirical patterns in my tests of Hypothesis 2. The other two top contributors—Bangladesh and India—are large-population states that are known to participate in peacekeeping as a form of jobs program (Perry and Smith 2013), again fitting the models analyzed above.

Which states contributed quickly to UNMIS? As mentioned above, UNMIS unrolled slowly. When the mission began in March 2005, it had received contributions from only eleven states. Egypt was one of these contributors. So was Kenya. In 2005, when the United Nations established UNMIS, Kenya hosted over 76,000 refugees from Sudan (UNHCR 2018). These large refugee inflows were of particular concern to Kenya because of its water scarcity issues. In the early 2000s, Kenya began to have high demand for freshwater from the Nile River Basin, given its recent population growth. Furthermore, 60 percent of its population lived in rural areas in which only a third of that population had access to improved water sources from the Nile Basin (FAO 2006; World Bank 2002). With the influx of these refugees into Kenya's rural borderlands with Sudan, the significant strain on its water supply increased dramatically. With the smallest military in the Nile Basin, intervention into the Sudanese conflict did not appear to be a feasible option for Kenya. However, once UNMIS was established, Kenya saw this operation as a solution to ending the refugee inflows from Sudan (Adar 2007). Kenya thus contributed troops to UNMIS beginning at the initiation of the mission. Several of the other initial contributors—Bangladesh, India, and Pakistan—were the expected large-population states that the UN frequently asks to participate in its operations. However, the role of colonial ties was also evident, as the United Kingdom joined the mission at its start. However, the United Kingdom also emphasized the importance of containing the conflict's refugee flows (SSFCA 2006).

Who withdrew early from UNMIS? Although UN Secretary-General Ban Ki-moon suggested an extension of UNMIS to allow for the resolution of the CPA's outstanding issues, Sudanese president al-Bashir requested that the UN withdraw as soon as South Sudan became independent on July 9, 2011. Until then, however, refugee outflows from Sudan continued despite the presence of UNMIS, with over 50,000 civilians displaced in 2008 alone. The continued violence, and associated displacement, meant that civilian protection remained a high priority for UNMIS forces throughout the CPA's implementation (Hansen 2015). Egypt and Kenya had different experiences. Although the Sudanese refugee population in Egypt remained stable over the course of the mission, it decreased in Kenya. However, both states remained committed to the mission. Remember, however, that increasing refugee inflows are most likely to drive away noncontiguous states that have little other interests in the conflict. This pattern was exhibited by Austria, whose Sudanese refugee population more than doubled over the course of UNMIS.

The case of UNMIS supports the results of the statistical analysis. Refugee inflows help shape a state's willingness to contribute to a United Nations peacekeeping mission. However, other strategic considerations are also important because states do not make the peacekeeping decision alone. Overall, however, one of the best ways the UN can overcome its dilemmas in attracting and mobilizing peacekeepers to a given mission is to allow those states most directly affected by the conflict to contribute to the mission as soon as possible.

The UN Multidimensional Integrated Stabilization Mission in Mali, 2013–Present

The econometric analysis given above is limited in temporal scope to 2015, due to data availability. Therefore, it may be helpful to consider an ongoing case to analyze whether the patterns captured in the data are still present today. The United Nations Multidimensional Integrated Stabilization Mission in Mali (MINUSMA) is one of the most recently established UN peacekeeping missions. It was established in 2013 (and thus is included in the data analysis), but it has not yet concluded, as of 2019. Examining MINUSMA is also helpful because this UN mission grew directly out of an ongoing African Union–ECOWAS mission. These regional organizations have their own members—which are also UN members—and their own institutional rules and procedures (namely, a standby force) that influence a state's participation in peace operations. As we will see in discussing MINUSMA, such institutional arrangements are particularly helpful for overcoming the dilemma of keeping member states committed to an ongoing mission.

In 2011, many ethnic Tuareg fighters, who had fought to support Muammar Gaddafi's regime as it collapsed in Libya, returned to their homes in northern Mali. Dissatisfied with the state of affairs at home, these groups formed the Movement for the National Liberation of Azawad (MNLA) and began protesting for change. By January 2012, the MNLA turned violent

and began pushing government forces out of the North. Dissatisfied with
the government's handling of the rebellion, soldiers led by Capitan Ama-
dou Sanogo overthrew the democratic regime and formed the National
Committee for Recovering Democracy and Restoring the State (Comité
national pour le redressement de la démocratie et la restauration de l'État,
CNRDRE). This coup was condemned by the African Union and the Economic Community of West African States, which offered to help mediate
a political compromise to the coup and ongoing civil war. But the new
government was uncooperative. Seizing on the dysfunction in the capital,
MNLA captured territory in the North roughly the size of France and
declared independence for the Republic of Azawad (see Haysom 2014).

Realizing they would need help in recapturing the North, the CNRDRE
turned to the AU and ECOWAS for help. The AU authorized ECOWAS
to form a peacekeeping mission through its Standby Force and appealed
to the United Nations for logistical and financial help in operating this
force. In reviewing this request, however, the UN was hesitant to support
the mission. While expressing grave concern at "the increasing number of
displaced persons and refugees" caused by the conflict and demanding that
the warring parties respect human rights and refugee law, the Security
Council declined to support the mission until "additional information has
been provided [by ECOWAS] regarding the objectives, means and modali-
ties of the envisaged deployment and other possible measures" (Security
Council 2012). Recognizing the risk of involving its members in this conflict, the Security Council was slow to support any rash action in the area
(Lotze 2015).

Later that same year, the AU and ECOWAS once more requested UN
authorization and involvement in the planned International Support Mission in Mali (AFISMA). Yet the secretary-general once more balked at the
African peacekeeping plan, unless the Security Council could impose tight
conditions on the mission. By the end of 2012, six months after AFISMA
was originally scheduled to deploy and with the Tuaregs now rapidly
approaching Mali's capital, the Security Council authorized and supported
AFISMA. Realizing that the mission was being deployed too late, the
CNRDRE asked Mali's former colonizer, France, to help defeat the rebels.
Within weeks, France had pushed the Tuaregs out of the major population
centers, and AFISMA was deployed. However, the CNRDRE was dissatisfied with AFISMA and asked that the UN take over peacekeeping in the
country. By mid-2013, the Security Council consented and formed
MINUSMA despite the objections of the AU and ECOWAS that "Africa

was not appropriately consulted" in the formation of the mission (African Union 2013). After strategically re-hatting the current forces of AFISMA as UN peacekeepers, the Security Council found only half of its mandated troop level filled. Furthermore, it lacked aviation capabilities among its contributing members, creating a major stumbling block at the onset of the mission (Lotze 2015).

MINUSMA's drawn-out formation process supports two important dynamics, which I highlighted in earlier chapters. First, the United Nations is aware that its member states are hesitant to support complex missions. The Security Council and secretary-general both hesitated to ask UN member states to support the AU–ECOWAS mission in Mali. Part of this hesitation was in the understanding that missions suffering from unclear objectives and planning would fail to garner members' support. Indeed, less than a year after forming MINUSMA, the United Nations convened the High-Level Independent Panel on Peace Operations (HIPPO 2015) to assess how missions could be better planned, made more effective, and better attract member participation. Second, given the tension between the Security Council's expanding expectations for peacekeeping missions and member states' interest in providing these services far abroad, mandates often go unfulfilled, decreasing the effectiveness of the mission. MINUSMA's complex mandate called for 11,200 military peacekeepers. Yet it began the mission with fewer than half of these requested troops. And though the Security Council later further increased the mandated number of troops, as of January 2019 MNUSMA was still understaffed (DPKO 2019).

When MINUSMA took over for AFISMA, the majority of the UN's peacekeeping force was made up of those African states that originally supported the AU–ECOWAS mission. At this point, the ten largest contributors were Benin, Burkina Faso, Chad, Ghana, Guinea, Côte d'Ivoire, Niger, Nigeria, Senegal, and Togo. Six of these top ten contributors were receiving refugees from Mali. Three of the four that had not yet experienced inflows—Ghana, Côte d'Ivoire, and Senegal—were members of ECOWAS's Standby Force and were participating as required by this membership. Chad was the only exception to these two forces driving participation early in the mission. However, it is important to note that Chad had entered the Mali conflict before the establishment of AFISMA as a military ally of France and supported the French in its military operation. Although the Security Council granted France special status to continue operating in Mali parallel to MINUSMA, Chad was integrated directly into the UN

Mission. Aside from these top ten contributors, and France, eight other UN members contributed at the start of this mission. Liberia was hosting Malian refugees and contributed significant troops to the mission. The other seven early contributors—which were a mixture of refugee hosts (e.g., Mauritania), ECOWAS members (e.g., Sierra Leone), large-population states (e.g., Bangladesh), and P5 members (e.g., Britain and the United States)—each only contributed nominally to the mission (between one and five soldiers). Here we again see the importance of refugee flows influencing overall patterns in which members contribute quickly to UN missions. The Mali case, however, also highlights the growing norm of regional actors working through non-UN organizations to help keep the peace before integrating with the United Nations (Bellamy and Williams 2005).

Over the six-year course of MINUSMA, the top contributors to the mission changed little. As of 2019, six of the top ten contributors remain the same as in 2013—Burkina Faso, Chad, Guinea, Niger, Senegal, and Togo. These patterns again highlight the importance of refugee flows in motivating not only whether a state participates in a mission but also how much it contributes. However, over the course of the mission, some change among the top contributors has occurred. Benin, Ghana, Côte d'Ivoire, and Nigeria no longer rank in the top ten. Now, Bangladesh, Egypt, Germany, and China have joined the top ranks. Part of this change is driven by factors shown to be important in the analysis given above. Bangladesh, for example, has used this mission as part of its peacekeeping-as-jobs program for its large population. However, other developing patterns appear for contributors to MINUSMA that are not captured in the models analyzed above. China, for instance, has expanded its role in peacekeeping in hopes of rebranding its international image. It is particularly interested in contributing to the most severe African conflicts, for two reasons. First, China has invested heavily in unstable African countries where Western finance hesitates to go. It sees its peacekeepers as essential to protecting its return on investment in these areas. Keeping peace in Mali is of particular concern to China because it fears that the Tuaregs will push their fight across the border into Niger, where China has invested heavily in mineral extraction (Savstrom 2018). Second, the severity of the conflict is appealing to China because it uses the peacekeeping missions as combat training for its military. Given its higher tolerance for casualties, China is able and willing to deploy to conflicts and areas that many Western states are not (Pauley 2018).

Early withdrawal has not been an issue with MINUSMA. Those states that hosted the most Malian refugees in 2013 when AFISMA was formed—Burkina Faso, Mauritania, and Niger—are the same states that host the most Malian refugees today (UNHCR 2018). Furthermore, these states have each contributed troops to peacekeeping in Mali from the beginning. The role of ECOWAS has been important to this dynamic. Unlike the United Nations, ECOWAS has a standing peacekeeping force designed for rapid and long-term deployment. Each of its member states is required to submit personnel to the standing force. When war erupted in Mali, the ECOWAS leadership saw the conflict in its member states as a direct threat to regional stability and worked quickly to provide political and military support in the situation (Haysom 2014). Committing its members' personnel to continued peacekeeping in Mali through its Standby Force, ECOWAS ensured long-term commitment from its members as long as the regional organization remained concerned about the refugee crisis and the potential for conflict diffusion. This institutional mechanism for ensuring member participation is something that the United Nations does not possess. As is clear from the cases of AFISMA and MINUSMA, regional organizations with such an institutional design can be crucial in helping the United Nations overcome the issues that continued refugee flows create for the stability of its missions.

It is important to note that though Burkina Faso and Niger are members of ECOWAS, Mauritania is not. Although each of these three states has contributed personnel throughout the duration of MINUSMA, two crucial patterns in their participation appear linked to the involvement of ECOWAS and its Standby Force. First, the participation of Burkina Faso and Niger in Mali predates that of Mauritania, as each of these states initially contributed personnel through ECOWAS in AFISMA. Second, though Burkina Faso and Niger have steadily been among the top contributors to both missions, Mauritania has not. Instead, Mauritania has made token contributions to the UN mission. Two points about this behavior are worth noting. First, as Mauritania is not a member of ECOWAS, it cannot be compelled to contribute in the same fashion as Burkina Faso and Niger. Second, Mauritania has hesitated to participate in the UN mission because it has been dissatisfied with how the United Nations has handled the Tuareg conflict. Mauritania believes that a tougher stance vis-à-vis the jihadist faction of the Tuareg rebels is needed. To this end, it has dedicated greater resources to the efforts of the G5 Sahel Joint Force it established in

2014 with Burkina Faso, Chad, Mali, and Niger to combat the jihadists. As of 2018, Mauritania also leads the group militarily by controlling the position of the joint force command. Seeing the G5 Sahel Force as a superior option to MINUSMA, Mauritanian president Mohamed Ould Abdel Aziz has openly criticized the UN mission and has called on the international community to further support the Sahel Force: "We don't understand why the international community continues to pour billions of dollars into MINUSMA without results while the five G5 countries . . . don't manage to raise even one-tenth of what goes every year to MINUSMA" (Kelly 2018).

Like Tanzania's use of the Force Intervention Brigade, given its dissatisfaction with UN peacekeeping in the DRC, Mauritania's Sahel Force is designed to be a more flexible foreign policy tool in achieving the country's goals in its neighbor. However, as with the Force Intervention Brigade in the DRC, the United Nations is working with the G5 to coordinate its efforts with the ongoing peacekeeping work (Kelly 2018). Mauritania's agitation is of concern to the UN because this political maneuvering in the region threatens to divert the personnel and attention of some of the top MINUSMA contributors. Niger, for instance, has already pledged over 1,000 troops—more than it has in MINUSMA—to the Sahel Force. Niger is a crucial ally for both the UN and Mauritania in the Mali conflict because of Niger's dedication to the fight. Possessing a significant Tuareg population in its northern territory, Niger has been dedicated to defeating the insurgency for fear that Tuareg success in Mali will spawn a Tuareg rebellion on its own borders (Haysom 2014). These developments within the G5 will provide a crucial test for the UN's ability to maintain its members' contributions and for ECOWAS's members' commitment to continuing the work started by its Standby Force through this institution.

The case of MINUSMA provided further support for my overall claim that refugee flows greatly influence how member states respond to the UN's calls for contributions to its peacekeeping missions. This case also highlights the important role regional organizations can have in sustaining UN peacekeeping activities. Of further importance, the MINUSMA case underscores that institutional design greatly shapes state behavior and has important implications for how peacekeeping unfolds and can be maintained. Unlike MONUC and UNMIS, MINUSMA has not had substantial issues with early withdrawal. The ability for the UN to overcome this issue in Mali is most likely due to its partnership with regional organizations that have Standby Force institutions. Though there have been calls for the

United Nations to develop similar institutions, such appeals have been fruitless to date.

Summary

The models presented in this chapter provide strong support for Hypotheses 1, 3, and 4. Overall, they support my specific claim that refugee flows help shape a member state's willingness to contribute to specific UN peacekeeping missions. They also support my broader claim that conflict- and mission-specific factors tend to outweigh the member-specific factors on which previous research has focused (e.g., democracy and poverty). However, besides direct refugee inflows, few factors have consistent effects on the dynamics of peacekeeping contribution along each of the dimensions considered. Table 3.5 presents a summary of the results found across the four analyses. From this summary, four general patterns emerge that speak to how the United Nations attracts, mobilizes, and retains support for its peacekeeping operations. First, conflict-specific factors matter. Specifically, the refugee crisis created by the conflict affects each stage of a mission. However, there is nuance in how the UN's member states respond to the organization's emphasis on protecting civilians. Although direct flows motivate members to participate quickly, these externalities can also break apart a mission's coalition of contributors if the operation does not halt the flow of refugees. Conversely, the total refugee flows produced by the mission mimic the effects of the direct flows in increasing participation (in some models), but member states are often slower to become involved in these conflicts. Members do, however, remain more committed to missions in countries that are continuing to produce large refugee outflows.

Second, traditional explanations for which states answer the UN's call to engage in peacekeeping find limited support. Though there is evidence that poor states are more likely to contribute than their wealthier peers (e.g., Victor 2010) and remain committed to the mission, there is limited evidence on whether they contribute more troops or do so quickly. Democracies are no more likely to participate than nondemocracies (see Lebovic 2004). Furthermore, there is limited evidence as to whether democracies provide more troops than other regimes or remain committed to the mission in which they are participating. However, my analysis has added nuance to our understanding of these regimes, as there is strong evidence that democracies tend to contribute quickly to UN peacekeeping missions. Third, military and colonial interests have a significant influence on which

Table 3.5.   Summarizing this Book's Findings

Variable	Likelihood of Participation	Size of Contribution	Quickness of Participation	Withdrawal of Contribution
Ln(Refugee Inflows)	Increases	No Effect	Increases	Increases
Ln(Total Refugee Outflows)	Increases#[a]	Increases#	Decreases#	Decreases
Democracy	No Effect	Increases#	Increases	Decreases#
Ln(GDPpc)	Decreases	Decreases#	Increases#	Increases
Ln(Population Size)	Increases	Increases	Increases	No Effect
P5	No Effect	No Effect	No Effect	Decreases#
Contiguous	Decreases#	Increases#	Decreases	No Effect
Joint Ethnicity	Decreases#	Decreases	Decreases#	Increases
Alliance	Increases	Increases#	Increases	No Effect
Colonial Ties	Increases	No Effect	Increases	No Effect
Ln(Other Contributors)	Increases	Decreases	Increases	Decreases

[a] Limited support is denoted by #.

states become involved in peacekeeping. Allies and former colonial powers are more likely to participate and contribute quickly to missions. There is some evidence that allies are also likely to contribute larger forces to these operations. However, neither type of state is likely to withdraw from the operation any sooner than other states. Interestingly, while these more traditional realpolitik interests help drive member states' behavior, there is much less evidence that local geopolitical factors, such as contiguity and ethnic kinship, influence member behavior regarding peacekeeping. However, some evidence suggests that joint ethnicity decreases a member's willingness to contribute substantially to a mission or remain committed throughout the operation. Finally, peacekeeping is clearly a collaborative effort. States help attract each other to missions quickly, and they help share the burden with one another. These patterns fit well with the UN's view of peacekeeping as a "global partnership" (DPKO 2018i).

Notes

1. These data have been updated to 2015 by Kathman since the original publication of the data set.

2. Descriptive statistics for the data are available in the supplemental materials found on the author's website, https://sites.google.com/site/uzonyigary/.

3. Goodness-of-fit statistics (Akaike's Information Criterion and the Bayesian Information Criterion) indicate that the ZINB is preferable to the standard negative binomial model.

4. The results given below for *Ln(Other Contributors)* hold if, instead, I also use the amount of troops that each of these other states contributes.

5. In a subsequent analysis, I also control for whether the war-torn state is hosting a non-UN mission simultaneously with the UN operation, as members may choose to contribute to this action instead. I find that my results are robust to the inclusion of this variable. This is most likely because though non-UN involvement may correlate with the presence of a UN mission, it does not correlate with whether any given UN member is receiving refugees (though it may correlate with the total number of refugees produced by the conflict).

6. All effect sizes from the probit model are calculated using King, Tomz, and Wittenberg's (2000) *Clarify*.

7. All further analyses are reported in the supplemental materials.

8. Effect sizes for the ZINB are produced using the Incident Rate Ratio.

9. Effect sizes for the duration model are produced from the Hazard Ratio.

4

Conclusion: Managing Incentives
and Disincentives to Keep the Peace

THE UNITED NATIONS faces three dilemmas in staffing its peacekeeping missions. First, given that the UN does not have a standing peacekeeping force, how can it convince its members to contribute military personnel to its missions? Second, how can the United Nations convince its members to contribute quickly to the missions it proposes before the situation in the target country deteriorates to the point where the UN is unable or unwilling to help manage the conflict? Third, once the operation deploys, how can the UN convince its members to remain committed to the mission until its goals are reached? Since the United Nations first deployed an operation in 1948, it has repeatedly reimagined the role and extent of its peacekeeping forces. Each shift in its peacekeeping focus has caused the intensity of these dilemmas, and how the UN attempts to overcome these problems, to ebb and flow. In this book, I consider how the UN handles these dilemmas in the post–Cold War era. I focus on how the increasingly humanitarian rhetoric of the UN connects with the military interests of some members to attract peacekeeping contributions from states that are experiencing direct refugee inflows from a mission's target state. Additionally, I explore how this particular motive to contribute troops to a specific mission can undermine the long-term commitment by those same host states.

Civilians and the United Nations:
Motive and Opportunity for Participation

In the post–Cold War era, and especially since 1999, the United Nations has come to emphasize the promotion of human rights and the protection of civilians through its peacekeeping missions. This shift has raised questions about how the UN will continue to staff its peacekeeping missions, given that most of these personnel have traditionally come from states with weak human rights enforcement and little concern for civilians. The fear is that such illiberal contributors would limit their participation in the UN's activities over concerns that their involvement could help set a precedent of the international community using peacekeeping to force states like them to change their domestic policies. This would be a direct threat to each government's jealously guarded sovereignty.

Often overlooked in these concerns, however, is the practical benefit that this shift in the UN's rhetoric to focusing on civilian protection has had in better connecting its normative institutional interests to the strategic or realpolitik interests of its member states. In emphasizing civilian protection, the UN's leadership has made clear the connection between civilian protection, the promotion of human rights, and stopping refugee flows. In Resolution 1674 (Security Council 2006), the Security Council emphasized protecting civilians and providing humanitarian assistance to create conditions to end forced migration and allow for the return of refugees. Secretary-General Ban Ki-moon (2007) highlighted refugees as a primary feature of contemporary conflicts, the challenge forced migration poses for the international community, and the potential usefulness of peacekeeping in ending these flows. Similarly, in Resolution 1894 (Security Council 2009), the Security Council noted the need to protect civilians early in the conflict as a way to avoid situations of significant forced migration. By emphasizing the connection between civilian protection and refugee flows, and making clear the usefulness of peacekeeping in ending these flows, the United Nations has given member states a way to sell their involvement in peacekeeping to their domestic constituents.

By connecting the protection of civilians, the promotion of human rights, and the stopping of refugee flows, the United Nations has also given leaders flexibility in how they sell their involvement in a mission. As discussed in chapter 2, US President Bill Clinton focused on refugee flows and their consequences to help sell US intervention in Haiti to the US public. However, the perception of the mighty United States being unable to keep

malnourished individuals—clinging to "flotillas" in the Gulf of Mexico—
from walking onto its shores turned off some voters. Clinton's campaign
strategists began fearing that the focus on the refugees was harming his
image. For instance, his strategist Dick Morris eventually suggested fram-
ing the refugee issue as a human rights issue, arguing to Clinton that "you
look weak when you are trying to stop refugees from flooding us, but
you look strong when you are protecting children abroad" (quoted by
Girard 2004, 71). Instead of dropping the refugee frame completely, Clinton
incorporated Morris's advice into his previous message and used both
frames together. Similarly, the leaders of NATO's member states connected intervention in the Balkans to both human rights and the refugee
flows that the Serbian conflicts were creating to sell the mission to their
constituents (Ignazi, Giacomello, and Coticchia 2012). Having the flexibility to move between similar messages until one strikes the right chord with
constituents is particularly useful to democratic leaders who must balance
the demands of different groups, urging action for either humanitarian or
security reasons (Western 2002).

Highlighting the strategic value of civilian protection for the UN in
terms of the hurdles it faces in convincing member states to participate in
peacekeeping missions is not meant to lessen the normative value of protecting human life; nor is it meant to ignore the military value of helping
to alleviate some of the causes of continued fighting. Instead, focusing on
this connection between the UN's shift in priorities to protecting civilians
and member states' willingness to contribute to peacekeeping efforts helps
reemphasize an important point about member state behavior—it is often
driven by the state's military and political interests. The case studies and
empirical analysis I have presented in the previous chapters make clear that
member states' interests regarding specific conflicts and peacekeeping missions help drive their participation in peacekeeping rather than an idealis-
tic commitment to certain normative values. Often, the normative concerns
voiced in the UN Charter and by the UN's leadership are discussed as if
they are at odds with strategic military and political issues. That is, an
action is either in favor of the Charter or it is in favor of realpolitik (Beardsley and Schmidt 2012). But it can be both.

Rather than support a theoretical divide between realist and liberal
views of institutions (Mearsheimer 1994), this project helps emphasize how
normative and positivist concerns can reinforce each other. The United
Nations clearly has normative, liberal interests in protecting civilian populations. Member states may also have normative interests in protecting

civilian populations. They also clearly have interests in stopping refugee inflows and repatriating those forced migrants who have entered the hosts' territory. Together, these normative and political interests motivate members to work with the UN toward the unified goal of protecting vulnerable populations. It also becomes clear that such a dyadic, conflict-specific approach to understanding peacekeeping behavior better explains patterns in participant behavior than the traditional monadic, member-specific approach. States that are receiving refugee inflows from a specific conflict are more likely to contribute to a peacekeeping mission addressing that crisis than are others. They are also likely to become involved more quickly, and to contribute more military personnel, than are others. Thus, this argument helps explain why weak and strong states, and democracies and nondemocracies, are all willing to participate in some peacekeeping missions but not in others.

Still, tension can exist between how the UN overcomes its initial two dilemmas of attracting participants and getting them to deploy quickly and its third dilemma of keeping states committed to the mission over time. Because these states are participating to accomplish a particular mission-specific goal in stopping forced migration from the target country, their expectations for the mission are often formed in relation to this policy goal. These states consider missions beneficial and successful if they reduce refugee inflows. The missions are largely a waste of time if the inflows continue. The member states interested in stopping inflows are unlikely to remain committed to the mission if they view it as unsuccessful. Therefore, the mechanism that helps pull members into a mission can be the same one that pushes them to withdraw. It is then the states that are more interested in the global, humanitarian aspect of the mission, that are often more hesitant to become involved, or those participating to export labor, that are left to help guide the target toward postconflict peace and stability. For example, Bangladesh, India, and Pakistan remain the top contributors to the UN's efforts in the Democratic Republic of Congo, despite MONUSCO's continued failures in maintaining peace and protecting civilians near the battle zones (DPKO 2018a).

Again, it is important to note that these patterns in how states react to the call for peacekeeping reveal that peacekeeping is not often a practice devoid of military logic. Instead, for many countries, UN peacekeeping provides a legitimizing cover and mechanism through which to aggregate their capabilities with other states to achieve their domestic and foreign policy goals in another country. For example, in the post–Cold War era,

Italy is hesitant to involve its military in actions that may be considered warlike. However, Italy is very willing to contribute its forces to multilateral missions, especially when these missions are under the auspices of an international organization that grants further legitimacy to the action (Ignazi, Giacomello, and Coticchia 2012). As the vast body of literature on military strategy clarifies, military intervention requires a motive and opportunity. For peacekeeping participation, the refugee inflows provide the motive and the United Nations provides the opportunity for involvement in war-torn states. The members then interpret, and react to, the motive and the opportunity on the basis of their domestic politics. For instance, democracies are hesitant to send their troops abroad, even for peacekeeping. My research thus highlights the need for scholars and observers to think more carefully about the military advantages and disadvantages the United Nations system presents to its member states.

Lessons Learned

The specific patterns of who contributes where, when, and for how long, given conflict- and mission-specific concerns, help us to also understand broader patterns within the UN system. In the post–Cold War era, the contribution of peacekeepers from European countries has decreased. Simultaneously, contributions from African and Asian countries have increased. Observers have generally suggested that these patterns are evidence of the UN broadening the base of its peacekeeping contributors (Perry and Smith 2013). However, a conflict-specific understanding of peacekeeping can also explain these patterns—in part. In the post–Cold War era, Africa and Asia have experienced more civil war and forced migration than Europe. In response, the UN has authorized more peacekeeping missions in these regions (DPKO 2018j). Following my logic, nearby refugee-receiving states have responded by contributing more military personnel to these missions to help decrease refugee flows into their territories (Kathman 2013). Recall from chapter 3, for instance, that Ethiopia rarely contributed to UN peacekeeping missions before the operations in Sudan and South Sudan.

Observers have also noted that the UN has increasingly attempted to shift the peacekeeping burden onto regional organizations (Bellamy and Williams 2005). The conflict-specific theory of peacekeeping I provide suggests a different understanding of these developments. Because states most directly affected by the conflict are those that are most likely to participate in helping resolve the crisis, nearby states and the regional organizations of which they are also members are the ones pushing to help their war-torn neighbors on their own regional terms. Recall that it was the Southern African Development Community that helped mediate the end of Africa's World War in the Democratic Republic of Congo, and that the community's members pushed for the resulting peacekeeping operations to be African driven. Similarly, Sudan's al-Bashir demanded that any peacekeeping mission in Sudan be African-led because his neighbors were more likely to understand the intricacies of the situation. In response to these developments, and in understanding these regional demands, the African Union has formed its Standby Force to be able to respond quickly to conflicts in the region. Therefore, rather than being a story about how the European-dominated United Nations is dumping the peacekeeping burden onto regional organizations, it appears that these organizations are doing exactly what my conflict-specific theory of peacekeeping predicts. They are getting involved most in those conflicts that affect them most.

Furthermore, anecdotal evidence suggests that the member states of these regional organizations participate within these institutions along the same lines as they do within the UN. For example, in 1990, the Economic Community of West African States (ECOWAS) decided to organize its own peacekeeping mission in Liberia (ECOMOG). In defending the creation of ECOMOG, and elaborating on why he planned to contribute troops to the operation, Sierra Leone's president, Joseph Momoh, highlighted the need to stop refugee flows from Liberia due to the turmoil they were creating within host states and the region. He stated, "The massive influx of refugees into our country with its attendant economic and social consequences is just one of the many grave responsibilities we are now called upon to shoulder [through ECOMOG]" (quoted by Gberie 2005, 57). Obed Asamoah, Ghana's foreign minister, made a similar claim. He argued that the heavy economic toll of the refugee situation on Liberia's neighbors made rapid intervention by ECOWAS an imperative (Adibe 1997). In fact, these concerns led ECOWAS to authorize its peacekeepers to use much more force than typically allowed by UN personnel. Rather than gaining the consent of the parties, remaining impartial, and avoiding force except in self-defense, ECOMOG forces actively fought in the war until the Abuja Accord was established and elections were held in 1997 (Ellis 1999).

Although strategic interests help bring participants into these missions, these same interests may lead to pathologies within the operation. In particular, these nonhumanitarian motivations may have implications for the at-risk civilian populations these states seek to prevent from exiting the conflict country. As third parties work to stop the flows of refugees from entering their territory, they may order their troops to use any means necessary to stop inflows from crossing their border, or they may also simply ignore abuses by their own troops. If the troops policing the inflows feel it necessary to use high levels of force to achieve their objectives, some states may be unlikely to flinch at these techniques. Evidence of such behavior is apparent in both the UN's current mission in the DRC (United Nations Organization Stabilization Mission in the Democratic Republic of the Congo, MONUSCO) as well as ECOMOG's involvement in Liberia. For example, in the DRC, the Tanzanian-led Force Intervention Brigade has indiscriminately bombed suspected rebel locations (Day 2017). Similarly, in Liberia, ECOMOG used indiscriminate bombing in the rebel-held territories and targeted some civilians directly (Human Rights Watch 1993). This behavior places the United Nations in a difficult position. It must balance the need for peacekeepers, and the willingness of security-motivated members to contribute, with the potential effects these contributions may have on its goals.

These dynamics are important for our understanding of international relations, as they highlight the importance of organizational design. Research on the United Nations and regional organizations tends to focus on how major powers can force multilateral organizations closer to their ideal policy points (Voeten 2001) and can legitimize their actions through the organization (Thompson 2009). Questions remain, however, about whether the major powers can maintain control of their projects once they are implemented by the organization and its smaller members, whose interests may not be aligned with those of the major powers. In the post–Cold War era, these questions center on the UN's ability to use peacekeeping to protect civilians, promote human rights, and democratize failing states (e.g., Ratner 1995). If participants in these missions are focused on their own aims of preventing refugee flows rather than on the UN's goals, it is not surprising that many of these missions fail in establishing long-lasting democracies with strong human rights records. Is also helps explain why the UN has had such mixed success in helping maintain postconflict peace (e.g., Rustad and Binningsbo 2012).

For the United Nations, this means that it must carefully consider member states' incentives for participating in peacekeeping. Rather than attempting to keep interested states from participating for fear of their ulterior motives and undue influence in the target states (Bellamy and

Williams 2005), the UN should work with these states to respond quickly to humanitarian crises while making sure an exit strategy exists that does not harm the national sovereignty and future political situations of the target states (Bueno de Mesquita and Downs 2006). Of course, this is easier said than done. One potential solution is to partner more effectively with the regional organizations that desire to make or keep the peace in a given conflict, and diversify the role of each organization. For example, the regional states could coordinate and conduct the initial operation when the conflict is of particular salience to them, while the United Nations could recruit large-population states from outside the region to provide a longer-term presence in the country with interests in the mission that are not tied to whether the refugee flows continue. This would allow the more motivated regional states to participate quickly and contribute substantially to the mission, while the United Nations more carefully and slowly negotiates long-term commitments from other member states. Those distant members could then provide the necessary sustained presence in country once the regional troops begin to withdraw.

Having a two-pronged approach would help the United Nations overcome the tensions that have been found in how it can best attract contributors quickly and significantly to a mission and then maintain the necessary long-term presence in the country for conflict management to be successful at helping ensure postconflict stability. Because refugee-focused contributors are likely to remain in country only as long as their mission-specific interests are being met, it is hard to foretell how long each of these states is likely to remain committed to the mission. Having a second wave of contributors whose participation is unconnected to their own goals vis-à-vis the target country helps ensure that as the original participants begin to withdraw, there will be states committed to remaining within the target state to help with the pains associated with the postconflict period.

One thing to consider is that my research has focused on why states contribute troops to peacekeeping missions. But UN missions also sometimes seek contributions of armed police officers and/or unarmed observers. I focus on troop provision because such contributions entail the most risk for the participating member states. Troops perform the riskiest and deadliest tasks. Provision of these individuals also means that the member state is unable to use them for its own national or regime security during their deployment. Furthermore, the UN's concerns about the underprovision of peacekeeping personnel often focuses on these boots on the ground. But the police and observers in peacekeeping missions also provide essential services to the maintenance of peace. Therefore, understanding the contributions of these personnel is also important. Following Hultman, Kathman, and Shannon (2013), I posit that troop contributions are costlier and riskier for members than the contributions of these other personnel. Because this risk is reduced through the provision of armed police or unarmed observers, I expect the UN to face a lower barrier in attracting contributions. In these cases, refugee inflows are still an important part of the participation decision, but to a lesser extent than troop contributions.

New Avenues of Research

Although I have contributed to a more complete understanding of the UN's ability to attract peacekeepers and to do so quickly by focusing on the selective benefits states receive directly from each given conflict, many additional avenues of research persist for future scholars. As we begin to open up a state's decision-making process on whether, where, and when to contribute peacekeeping troops to humanitarian crises, several new questions arise. A first set of questions focuses on how the UN Security Council responds when it has difficulty attracting member states to contribute quickly to a potential peace operation. Does this delay the formation of the operation? Does the Security Council scale down the proposed mission's mandate? A second set of questions focuses on the growth in non-UN peacekeeping missions. How do member states choose between contributing to a UN mission and contributing to a non-UN mission? Are the determinants of peacekeeping contributions and their timing the same for UN and non-UN missions? A final set of questions focuses on the effects of peacekeeping missions. What repercussions do target states face for having strong, wealthy, and motivated states enter their territories under the auspices of the United Nations? Do missions heavily weighted with such international muscle do a better job of keeping the peace? Do they make the target states more dependent on international help than in situations where fewer powerful states become involved?

It is clear from the recent historical record that the United Nations is taking more of an interest in the protection of civilians during civil wars and in their immediate aftermaths. A growing body of literature also suggests that the UN is having increasing success with this evolving goal (e.g., Hultman, Kathman, and Shannon 2013). However, for the UN to have continued success in protecting civilian populations, it will need to successfully attract willing and able members to contribute military personnel to its missions. This may be a big ask for the UN, and other regional organizations, during humanitarian crises when the combatants are particularly willing to target the peacekeepers. Yet these are the situations in which there is the greatest need for members to contribute personnel. Clearly, this is an important issue that scholars should continue to research in order to provide the best understanding of these dynamics to policymakers interested in protecting civilian populations.

References

Adar, Korwa. 2007. "Kenya's Foreign Policy and Geopolitical Interests." *African Sociological Review* 11, no. 1: 63–80.

Adelman, Howard, and Govind Rao. 2004. *War and Peace in Zaire/Congo: Analyzing and Evaluating Intervention, 1996–1997.* Trenton: Africa World Press.

Adeyemi, Segun. 2001. "Sierra Leone: Nigeria Threatens to Withdraw Troops from UNAMSIL". *All Africa*, April 16. http://allafrica.com/stories/2001041 80235.html.

Adibe, Clement. 1997. "The Liberia Conflict and the ECOWAS-UN Partnership." *Third World Quarterly* 18, no. 3: 471–88.

African Union. 2013. "Communiqué of the 371st Meeting of the Peace and Security Council of the African Union." PSC/PR/COMM. (CCCLXXI), 25 April.

Amnesty International. 2014. "Left Out in the Cold: Syrian Refugees Abandoned by the International Community." December 5. www.amnesty.org/en/docu ments/MDE24/047/2014/en/.

Anderlini, Sanam. 2017. "UN Peacekeepers' Sexual Assault Problem." *Foreign Affairs*, June 9. www.foreignaffairs.com/articles/world/2017-06-09/un-peace keepers-sexual-assault-problem.

Arkes, Hal, and Catherine Blumer. 1985. "The Psychology of Sunk Cost." *Organizational Behavior and Human Decision Processes* 35, no. 1: 124–40.

Associated Press. 2007. "GI's Gear Costs 100 Times More than in WWII." NBC, October 2. www.nbcnews.com/id/21105586/ns/us_news-military/t/gis-gear -costs-times-more-wwii/#.WilUHkqnG71.

Balch-Lindsay, Dylan, and Andrew Enterline. 2000. "Killing Time: The World Politics of Civil War Duration." *International Studies Quarterly* 44, no. 4: 615–42.

Ban Ki-moon. 2007. "Report of the Secretary-General on the Protection of Civilian in Armed Conflict." New York: United Nations.

———. 2011. "Remarks to Security Council's Open Debate on the Protection of Civilians in Armed Conflict." United Nations. www.un.org/apps/news/info cus/sgspeeches/search_full.asp?.statID--1371.

Beardsley, Kyle. 2011. "Peacekeeping and the Contagion of Armed Conflict." *Journal of Politics* 73, no. 4: 1051–64.

Beardsley, Kyle, and Holger Schmidt. 2012. "Following the Flag or Following the Charter? Examining the Determinants of UN Involvement in International Crises, 1945–2002." *International Studies Quarterly* 56, no. 1: 33–49.

Bellamy, Alex, and Paul Williams. 2005. "Who's Keeping the Peace? Regionalization and Contemporary Peace Operations." *International Security* 29, no. 4: 157–95.

———. 2013. *Providing Peacekeepers: The Politics, Challenges, and Future of United Nations Peacekeeping Contributions.* Oxford: Oxford University Press.

Bellamy, Alex, Paul Williams, and Stuart Griffin. 2004. *Understanding Peacekeeping.* Cambridge: Polity.

Bennett, D. Scott, and Alan Stam. 2000. "EUGene: A Conceptual Manual." *International Interactions* 26, no. 2: 179–204.

Berdal, Mats. 2013. "The United Nations, Peacekeeping and Power Politics." Geneva Centre for Security Policy. www.files.ethz.ch/isn/163961/Mats%20 Berdal%20Final.pdf.

Berman, Eric, and Katie Sams. 2000. *Peacekeeping in Africa: Capabilities and Culpabilities.* Geneva: United Nations Institute for Disarmament Research and Institute for Security Studies.

Blum, Andrew. 2000. "Blue Helmets from the South: Accounting for the Participation of Weaker States in United Nations Peacekeeping Operations." *Journal of Conflict Studies* 20, no. 1: 1–22.

Bobrow, David, and Mark Boyer. 1997. "Maintaining System Stability: Contributions to Peacekeeping Operations. *Journal of Conflict Resolution* 41, no. 6: 723–48.

Bolt, Jutta, Robert Inklaar, Herman de Jong, and Jan Luiten van Zanden. 2018. "Rebasing 'Maddison': New Income Comparisons and the Shape of Long-Run Economic Development." Maddison Project Working Paper. https://www.rug .nl/ggdc/historicaldevelopment/maddison/releases/maddison-project-data base-2018.

Boutros-Ghali, Boutros. 1999. *Unvanquished: A US-UN Saga.* London: I. B. Tauris.

Bove, Vincenzo, and Leandro Elia. 2011. "Supplying Peace: Participation in and Troop Contribution to Peacekeeping Missions." *Journal of Peace Research* 48, no. 6: 699–714.

Brahimi, Lakhdar. 2000. "Report of the Panel on United Nations Peace Operations." New York: United Nations.

Bueno de Mesquita, Bruce, and George Downs. 2006. "Intervention and Democracy." *International Organization* 60, no. 3: 627–49.

Bueno de Mesquita, Bruce, and Randolph Siverson. 1995. "War and the Survival of Political Leaders: A Comparative Study of Regime Types and Political Accountability." *American Political Science Review* 89, no. 4: 841–55.

Cederman, Lars-Erik, and Manuel Vogt. 2017. "Dynamics and Logics of Civil War." *Journal of Conflict Resolution* 61, no. 9: 1992–2016.

Central Intelligence Agency. 2018. "World Factbook." www.cia.gov/library/publications/the-world-factbook/.

Choi, Seung-Whan. 2013. "What Determines US Humanitarian Intervention?" *Conflict Management and Peace Science* 30, no. 2: 121–39.

Cilliers, Jakkie, and Mark Malan. 2001. "Peacekeeping in the DRC." Institute for Security Studies, Africa.

Cingranelli, David, David Richards, and K. Chad Clay. 2014. "The CIRI Human Rights Dataset." Cingranelli-Richards Human Rights Data Project. https://www.humanrightsdata.com.

Dallaire, Roméo. 2009. *Shake Hands with the Devil: The Failure of Humanity in Rwanda*. New York: Random House.

Daniel, Donald. 2011. "Partnering for Troop Supply." *International Peacekeeping* 18, no. 5: 534–60.

Daniel, Donald, Patricia Taft, and Sharon Wiharta. 2008. *Peace Operations: Trends, Progress, and Prospects*. Washington, DC: Georgetown University Press.

Day, Adam. 2017. "The Best Defense Is No Offense: Why Cuts to UN Troops in Congo Could Be a Good Thing." *Small Wars Journal*, no date. http://smallwarsjournal.com/jrnl/art/the-best-defense-is-no-offense-why-cuts-to-un-troops-in-congo-could-be-a-good-thing.

Department of State. 1995. "The United Nations: The Momentum for Reform Must Accelerate." *Bureau of Public Affairs Dispatch* 6, no. 40.

Deutsche Presse Agentur. 2005. "Egyptian Parliament Approves Sending Peacekeeping Troops to Sudan." May 23. https://reliefweb.int/report/sudan/egyptian-parliament-approves-sending-peacekeeping-troops-sudan.

Diehl, Paul. 2008. *Peace Operations*. Malden, MA: Polity.

Doyle, Michael, and Nicholas Sambanis. 2006. *Making War and Building Peace*. Princeton, NJ: Princeton University Press.

DPKO (UN Department of Peacekeeping Operations). 2008. *Principles and Guidelines*. New York: United Nations.

———. 2014. *Background Note*. New York: United Nations.

———. 2017. "Our History." United Nations. https://peacekeeping.un.org/en/our-history.

———. 2018a. "Data." United Nations. https://peacekeeping.un.org/en/data.

———. 2018b. "Deployment and Reimbursement." United Nations. https://peacekeeping.un.org/en/deployment-and-reimbursement.

———. 2018c. "Haiti." https://peacekeeping.un.org/sites/default/files/past/unmih backgr2.html.

———. 2018d. "Our Successes." United Nations. https://peacekeeping.un.org/en /our-successes.

———. 2018e. "Promoting Human Rights." United Nations. https://peacekeeping .un.org/en/promoting-human-rights.

———. 2018f. "Protecting Civilians." United Nations. https://peacekeeping.un .org/en/protecting-civilians.

———. 2018g. "Reforming Peacekeeping." United Nations. https://peacekeeping .un.org/en/reforming-peacekeeping.

———. 2018h. "What We Do." United Nations. https://peacekeeping.un.org/en /what-we-do.

———. 2018i. "What Is Peacekeeping?" https://peacekeeping.un.org/en/what-is -peacekeeping.

———. 2018j. "Where We Operate." United Nations. https://peacekeeping.un .org/en/where-we-operate.

———. 2019. "MINUSMA." United Nations. https://peacekeeping.un.org/en /mission/minusma.

Dunham, Will. 2014. "Kerry Condemns Russia's Incredible Act of Aggression in Ukraine." Reuters. March 2. www.reuters.com/article/us-ukraine-crisis-usa -kerry/kerry-condemns-russias-incredible-act-of-aggression-in-ukraine -idUSBREA210DG20140302.

Durall, Julia. 2013. "United Nations Peacekeeping Operations under Chapter VII." *Revista del Instituto Espanol de Estudios Estrategicos* 2: 1–26.

Ellis, Stephen. 1999. *The Mask of Anarchy*. London: Hurst.

Essa, Azad. 2017a. "Is the UN Doing Enough to Stop Peacekeeper Abuse?" Al Jazeera, August 6. www.aljazeera.com/indepth/features/2017/07/stop-peace keeper-abuse-170730125107601.html.

———. 2017b. "UN Peacekeepers Hit by New Allegations of Sex Abuse." Al Jazeera, July 10. www.aljazeera.com/news/2017/07/peacekeepers-hit-allegations -sex-abuse-170701133655238.html.

FAO (Food and Agriculture Organization of the United Nations). 2006. *Statistical Yearbook*. Rome: FAO.

Fearon, James. 1997. "Signaling Foreign Policy Interests: Tying Hands versus Sinking Costs." *Journal of Conflict Resolution* 41, no. 1: 68–90.

Findley, Michael, and Tze Teo. 2006. "Rethinking Third-Party Intervention into Civil Wars: An Actor-Centric Approach." *Journal of Politics* 68, no. 4: 828–37.

Fortna, Virginia. 2008. *Does Peacekeeping Work? Shaping Belligerents' Choices after Civil War*. Princeton, NJ: Princeton University Press.

———. 2015. "Do Terrorists Win? Rebels' Use of Terrorism and Civil War Out-comes." *International Organization* 69, no. 3: 519–56.

Gberie, Lansana. 2005. *A Dirty War in West Africa: The RUF and the Destruction of Sierra Leone*. London: Hurst.

Gent, Stephen. 2007. "Strange Bedfellows: The Strategic Dynamics of Major Power Military Interventions." *Journal of Politics* 69, no. 4: 1089–1102.

———. 2008. "Going in When It Counts: Military Intervention and the Outcome of Civil Conflicts." *International Studies Quarterly* 52, no. 4: 713–35.

Ghobarah, Hazem, Paul Huth, and Bruce Russett. 2004. "Comparative Public Health: The Political Economy of Human Misery and Well-Being." *International Studies Quarterly* 48, no. 1: 73–94.

Gibbs, David. 1987. "Does the USSR Have a Grand Strategy? Reinterpreting the Invasion of Afghanistan." *Journal of Peace Research* 24, no. 4: 365–79.

———. 1997. "Is Peacekeeping a New Form of Imperialism?" *International Peacekeeping* 4, no. 1: 122–28.

Gibler, Douglas. 2009. *International Military Alliances, 1648–2008*. Thousand Oaks, CA: CQ Press.

Girard, Philippe. 2004. *Clinton in Haiti: The 1994 US Invasion of Haiti*. Berlin: Springer.

Gleason-Roberts, Megan. 2012. *Annual Review of Global Peace Operations*. New York: Center on International Cooperation.

Guardian. 2017. "The Observer View on Europe's Shameful Response to the Growing Refugee Crisis." July 8. www.theguardian.com/world/2017/jul/09 /observer-editorial-europes-shameful-response-to-growing-refugee-crisis.

Hafner-Burton, Emilie. 2008. "Sticks and Stones: Naming and Shaming the Human Rights Enforcement Problem." *International Organization* 62, no. 4: 689–716.

Hansen, Wibke. 2015. "United Nations Mission in Sudan (UNMIS)." In *The Oxford Handbook of United Nations Peacekeeping Operations*. Edited by Joachim Koops, Norrie Macqueen, Thierry Tardy, and Paul Williams. Oxford: Oxford University Press.

Haysom, Simone. 2014. *Security and Humanitarian Crisis in Mali: The Role of Regional Organisations*. HPG Working Paper. London: Overseas Development Institute.

Henke, Marina. 2016. "Great Powers and UN Force Generation: A Case Study of UNAMID." *International Peacekeeping* 23, no. 3: 468–92.

HIPPO (High-Level Independent Panel on Peace Operations). 2015. *The Future of United Nations Peace Operations: Implementation of the Recommendations of the High-Level Independent Panel on Peace Operations—Report of the Secretary-General*. New York: United Nations. https://digitallibrary.un.org/record/802167 /files/A_70_357_S_2015_682-EN.pdf.

Hultman, Lisa, Jacob Kathman, and Megan Shannon. 2013. "United Nations Peacekeeping and Civilian Protection in Civil War." *American Journal of Political Science* 57, no. 4: 875–91.

Human Rights Watch. 1993. "Liberia: Waging War to Keep the Peace." Report 5, no. 6.

———. 2003. "HRW World Report." www.hrw.org/legacy/wr2k3/.

Ignazi, Piero, Giampiero Giacomello, and Fabrizio Coticchia. 2012. *Italian Military Operations Abroad: Just Don't Call It War*. New York: Palgrave.

Integrated Regional Information Network. 2001. "IRIN-CEA Weekly Round-Up." United Nations Office for the Coordination of Humanitarian Affairs.

International Criminal Court. 2011. "Elements of Crimes." www.icc-cpi.int/NR /rdonlyres/336923D8-A6AD-40EC-AD7B-45BF9DE73D56/0/ElementsOf CrimesEng.pdf.

Iqbal, Zaryab, and Christopher Zorn. 2010. "Violent Conflict and the Spread of HIV/AIDS in Africa." *Journal of Politics* 72, no. 1: 149–62.

Jenkins, J. Craig, Stephen Scanlan, and Lindsey Peterson. 2007. "Military Famine, Human Rights, and Child Hunger." *Journal of Conflict Resolution* 51, no. 6: 823–47.

Jett, Dennis. 2000. *Why Peacekeeping Fails*. New York: St. Martin's Press.

Kathman, Jacob. 2011. "Civil War Diffusion and Regional Motivations for Intervention." *Journal of Conflict Resolution* 55, no. 6: 847–76.

———. 2013. "United Nations Peacekeeping Personnel Commitments, 1990–2011." *Conflict Management and Peace Science* 30, no. 5: 532–49.

Kathman, Jacob, and Molly Melin. 2016. "Who Keeps the Peace? Understanding State Contributions to UN Peacekeeping Operations." *International Studies Quarterly* 61, no. 1: 150–62.

Kathman, Jacob, and Reed Wood. 2011. "Managing Threat, Cost, and Incentive to Kill: The Short- and Long-Term Effects of Intervention in Mass Killings." *Journal of Conflict Resolution* 55, no. 5: 735–60.

Kelly, Fergus. 2018. "G5 Sahel Joint Force Better than UN's MINUSMA, Mauritania President Says." *Defense Post*, November 21. https://thedefensepost .com/2018/11/21/g5-sahel-joint-force-better-than-minusma-mauritania -president/.

King, Gary, Michael Tomz, and Jason Wittenberg. 2000. "Making the Most of Statistical Analyses." *American Journal of Political Science* 44, no. 2: 341–55.

Koch, Michael, and Scott Gartner. 2005. "Casualties and Constituencies: Democratic Accountability, Electoral Institutions, and Costly Conflicts." *Journal of Conflict Resolution* 49, no. 6: 874–94.

Krain, Matthew. 1997. "State-Sponsored Mass Murder: The Onset and Severity of Genocides and Politicides." *Journal of Conflict Resolution* 41, no. 3: 331–60.

Kreps, Sarah. 2007. "The 1994 Haiti Intervention: A Unilateral Operation in Multilateral Clothes." *Journal of Strategic Studies* 30, no. 3: 449–74.

Landman, Todd. 2005. *Protecting Human Rights: A Comparative Study*. Washington, DC: Georgetown University Press.

Lebovic, James. 2004. "Uniting for Peace? Democracies and United Nations Peace Operations after the Cold War." *Journal of Conflict Resolution* 48, no. 6: 910–36.

Leck, Christopher. 2009. "International Responsibility in United Nations Peace-keeping Operations." *Melbourne Journal of International Law* 10: 346–65.

Loescher, Gil, and James Milner. 2005. "The Long Road Home: Protracted Refu-gee Situations in Africa." *Survival* 47, no. 2: 153–74.

Lotze, Walter. 2015. "United Nations Multidimensional Integrated Stabilization Mission in Mali (MINUSMA)." In *The Oxford Handbook of United Nations Peacekeeping Operations*. Edited by Joachim Koops, Norrie Macqueen, Thierry Tardy, and Paul Williams. Oxford: Oxford University Press.

Marshall, Monty. 2009. "Forcibly Displaced Population." Center for Systemic Peace. www.systemicpeace.org/inscrdata.html.

Marshall, Monty, Ted Gurr, and Keith Jaggers. 2017. "Polity IV Project." Center for Systemic Peace. www.systemicpeace.org/inscrdata.html.

Marten, Kimberly. 2004. *Enforcing the Peace: Learning from the Imperial Past.* New York: Columbia University Press.

Mearsheimer, John. 1994. "The False Promise of International Institutions." *International Security* 19, no. 3: 5–49.

Meisler, Stanley. 1994. "UN Considers Withdrawal of Force in Rwanda." *Los Angeles Times*, April 14. http://articles.latimes.com/print/1994-04-14/news/mn-45819_1_u-n-peacekeeping-force.

Minde, Nicodemus. 2016. "Contributor Profile: Tanzania." International Law and Policy Institute, Oslo.

Moloo, Zahra. 2016. "UN Peacekeepers in the DRC No Longer Trusted to Pro-tect." Al Jazeera, January 18. www.aljazeera.com/indepth/features/2016/01/peacekeepers-drc-longer-trusted-protect-160112081436110.html.

Moore, Will, and Stephen Shellman. 2004. "Fear of Persecution: Forced Migration 1952–1995." *Journal of Conflict Resolution* 48, no. 5: 723–45.

———. 2007. "Whither Will They Go? A Study of Refugees' Destinations, 1965–1995." *International Studies Quarterly* 51, no. 4: 811–34.

Mueller, John. 2004. *The Remnants of War.* Ithaca, NY: Cornell University Press.

Murdoch, James, and Todd Sandler. 2004. "Civil Wars and Economic Growth: Spatial Dispersion." *American Journal of Political Science* 48, no. 1: 138–51.

Neack, Laura. 1995. "UN Peacekeeping: In the Interest of Community or Self?" *Journal of Peace Research* 32, no. 2: 181–96.

Olson, Mancur. 1965. *Logic of Collective Action.* Cambridge, MA: Harvard University Press.

Packenham, Robert. 2015. *A Liberal America and the Third World: Political Development Ideas in Foreign Aid and Social Science.* Princeton, NJ: Princeton University Press.

Pan-African News Agency. 2000. "ECOWAS Renews Call for Change in UNAMSIL Mandate." July 15. https://reliefweb.int/report/sierra-leone/ecowas-renews-call-change-unamsil-mandate.

Pauley, Logan. 2018. "China Takes the Lead in UN Peacekeeping." *The Diplomat*, April 17. https://thediplomat.com/2018/04/china-takes-the-lead-in-un-peacekeeping/.

Perry, Chris, and Adam Smith. 2013. "Trends in Uniform Contributions to UN Peacekeeping." *Providing for Peacekeeping* 3: 1–11.

Prunier, Gérard. 2009. *From Genocide to Continental War: The Congolese Conflict and the Crisis of Contemporary Africa.* London: Hurst.

Ramalho, Antonio, and Sanilo Marcondes de Souza Neto. 2015. "United Nations Mission in Haiti (UNMIH)." In *The Oxford Handbook of United Nations Peacekeeping Operations.* Edited by Joachim Koops, Norrie Macqueen, Thierry Tardy, and Paul Williams. Oxford: Oxford University Press.

Ratner, Steven. 1995. *The New UN Peacekeeping: Building Peace in Lands of Conflict after the Cold War.* New York: St. Martin's Press.

Regan, Patrick. 1998. "Choosing to Intervene: Outside Interventions in Internal Conflicts." *Journal of Politics* 60, no. 3: 754–79.

Reiter, Dan, and Allan Stam. 1998. "Democracy and Battlefield Military Effectiveness." *Journal of Conflict Resolution* 42, no. 3: 259–77.

Roberts, Adam. 1993. "Humanitarian War: Military Intervention and Human Rights." *International Affairs* 69, no. 3: 429–49.

Russett, Bruce, and John Oneal. 2001. *Triangulating Peace: Democracy, Interdependence, and International Organizations.* New York: W. W. Norton.

Rustad, Siri, and Helga Binningsbo. 2012. "A Price Worth Fighting For? Natural Resources and Conflict Recurrence." *Journal of Peace Research* 49, no. 4: 531–46.

Saideman, Stephen, and R. William Ayres. 2000. "Determining the Causes of Irredentism: Logit Analyses of Minorities at Risk Data from the 1980s and 1990s." *Journal of Politics* 62, no. 4: 1126–44.

Salehyan, Idean. 2008. "The Externalities of Civil Strife: Refugees as a Source of International Conflict." *American Journal of Political Science* 52, no. 4: 787–801.

Salehyan, Idean, and Kristian Gleditsch. 2006. "Refugees and the Spread of Civil War." *International Organization* 60, no. 2: 335–66.

Salverda, Nynke. 2013. "Blue Helmets as Targets: A Quantitative Analysis of Rebel Violence against Peacekeepers, 1989–2003." *Journal of Peace Research* 50, no. 6: 707–20.

Savstrom, Johan. 2018. "Self-Interest behind Shift of China's African Policy." Nordic African Institute, February 20. https://nai.uu.se/news/articles/2018/02/20/095540/index.xml.

Security Council. 1992. "Resolution 794." United Nations. https://documents-dds-ny.un.org/doc/UNDOC/GEN/N92/772/11/PDF/N9277211.pdf?OpenElement.

———. 1999a. "Resolution 1265." United Nations. https://documents-dds-ny.un.org/doc/UNDOC/GEN/N99/267/94/PDF/N9926794.pdf?OpenElement.

———. 1999b. "Resolution 1270." United Nations. https://documents-dds-ny.un.org/doc/UNDOC/GEN/N99/315/02/PDF/N9931502.pdf?OpenElement.

———. 2000. *Fifth Report of the Secretary-General on the United Nations Organization Mission in the Democratic Republic of the Congo.* New York: United Nations.

———. 2001. *Report of the Security Council Mission to the Great Lakes Region, 15–26 May 2011.* New York: United Nations.

———. 2006. "Resolution 1674." United Nations. www.un.org/ruleoflaw/files/S
-Res-1674%20on%20protection%20civilians%20in%20armed%20conflict%20
(28Apr06).pdf.

———. 2009. "Resolution 1894." United Nations. www.un.org/ruleoflaw/files
/Security%20Council%20Resolution%201894.pdf.

———. 2010. "Resolution 1925." United Nations. www.securitycouncilreport
.org/atf/cf/%7B65BFCF9B-6D27-4E9C-8CD3-CF6E4FF96FF9%7D/DRC
%20S%20RES%201925.pdf.

———. 2012. "Resolution 2056." United Nations. http://unscr.com/en/resolutions
/doc/2056.

———. 2017. *Report of the Secretary-General on the Implementation of Peace, Security and Cooperation Framework for the Democratic Republic of the Congo and the Region.* New York: United Nations.

Siverson, Randolph, and Harvey Starr. 1990. "Opportunity, Willingness, and the Diffusion of War." *American Political Science Review* 84, no. 1: 47–67.

Smith, Alastair. 1998. "International Crises and Domestic Politics." *American Political Science Review* 92: 623–38.

SSFCA (Office of the UK Secretary of State for Foreign and Commonwealth Affairs). 2006. *The United Kingdom in the United Nations.* Norwich: HMSO.

Stone, Jon. 2016. "Syrian Refugee Crisis: How Different Countries Have Responded." *Independent*, September 1. www.independent.co.uk/news/uk/politics/syrian
-refugee-crisis-how-different-countries-have-responded-france-lebanon-uk-a7
220616.html.

Tardy, Thierry. 2011. "A Critique of Robust Peacekeeping in Contemporary Peace Operations." *International Peacekeeping* 18, no. 2: 152–67.

Thompson, Alexander. 2009. *Channels of Power: The UN Security Council and US Statecraft in Iraq.* Ithaca, NY: Cornell University Press.

Tir, Jaroslav, Philip Schafer, Paul Diehl, and Gary Goertz. 1998. "Territorial Changes, 1816–1996: Procedures and Data." *Conflict Management and Peace Science* 16, no. 1: 89–97.

UN (United Nations). 2017. "ONUMOZ Background." https://peacekeeping.un
.org/sites/default/files/past/onumozFT.htm.

———. 2018a. "UNAMIR Background." https://peacekeeping.un.org/sites/default
/files/past/unamirFT.htm.

———. 2018b. "UNOSOM II Background." https://peacekeeping.un.org/sites
/default/files/past/unosom2backgr2.html.

———. 2018c. "UNPROFOR Background." https://peacekeeping.un.org/sites
/default/files/past/unprof_b.htm.

UNHCR (Office of the United Nations High Commissioner for Refugees). 2000. *The State of the World's Refugees.* New York: United Nations.

————. 2012. "One Year On, Somali Exodus Continues amid Conflict and Poor Rains." www.unhcr.org/cgi-bin/texis/vtx/search?page=search&docid=4fcdda ac9&query=dadaab.

————. 2017. *Global Trends: Forced Displacement in 2016*. New York: United Nations.

————. 2018. "Data." http://data.un.org/Data.aspx?d=UNHCR&f=indID%3AType -Ref.

Uzonyi, Gary. 2014. "Unpacking the Effect of Genocide and Politicide on Forced Migration." *Conflict Management and Peace Science* 31, no. 3: 225–43.

Victor, Jonah. 2010. "African Peacekeeping in Africa: Warlord Politics, Defense Economics, and State Legitimacy." *Journal of Peace Research* 47, no. 2: 217–29.

Voeten, Erik. 2001. "Outside Options and the Logic of Security Council Actions." *American Political Science Review* 95, no. 4: 845–58.

Walter, Barbara. 2009. "Bargaining Failures and Civil War." *Annual Review of Political Science* 12: 243–61.

Weiner, Myron. 1996. "Bad Neighbors, Bad Neighborhoods: An Inquiry into the Causes of Refugee Flows." *International Security* 21, no. 1: 5–42.

Wells, Matthew. 2016. "Casualties, Regime Type and the Outcomes of Wars of Occupations." *Conflict Management and Peace Science* 33, no. 5: 469–90.

Western, Jon. 2002. "Sources of Humanitarian Intervention: Beliefs, Intervention, and Advocacy in the US Decisions on Somalia and Bosnia." *International Security* 26, no. 4: 112–42.

White House. 1994. "Office of the Press Secretary, Selected Remarks Prepared for Delivery by President William Jefferson Clinton on US Policy toward Haiti, 15 September." www.presidency.ucsb.edu/ws/?pid=49093.

Willmot, Haidi, Ralph Mamiya, Scott Sheeran, and Marc Weeler. 2016. *Protection of Civilians*. Oxford: Oxford University Press.

World Bank. 2002. *World Development Indicators*. Washington, DC: World Bank.

————. 2015. *Turkey's Response to the Syrian Refugee Crisis and the Road Ahead*. Washington, DC: World Bank.

About the Author

Gary Uzonyi earned his PhD in political science from the University of Michigan (2013). His research interests focus on political violence and the international community response to it. He is currently an assistant professor at the University of Tennessee, Knoxville.